THE SHORTEST

"Beautifully and sparely constructed, yet rich in fact, feeling, and detail, sweeping, challenging, and funny."
—**James Button, award-winning journalist**

"A wise, illuminating little book."
—**Peter Craven, *Sydney Morning Herald***

"Crisp, lucid, and evocative prose … The balance of analysis and description, generalization, and specific instance, is beautifully maintained."
—**Wilfrid Prest, *Australian Book Review***

"An entertaining, learned piece of historical compression."
—***The Age***

"Great stuff, the book as a whole is constantly thought-provoking."
—***Courier Mail***

THE
SHORTEST
HISTORY
OF
EUROPE

**How Conquest, Culture, and
Religion Forged a Continent—
A Retelling for Our Times**

JOHN HIRST

Afterword by Filip Slaveski, PhD

THE EXPERIMENT
NEW YORK

The Experiment, LLC
220 East 23rd Street, Suite 600
New York, NY 10010-4658
theexperimentpublishing.com

The Experiment's books are available at special discounts when purchased in bulk for premiums and sales promotions as well as for fundraising or educational use. For details, contact us at info@theexperimentpublishing.com.

Library of Congress Cataloging-in-Publication Data

Names: Hirst, John (John Bradley), 1942-2016, author. | Slaveski, Filip, writer of afterword
Title: The shortest history of Europe : how conquest, culture, and religion forged a continent / John Hirst ; afterword by Filip Slaveski, PhD.
Description: Revised [edition]. | New York : The Experiment, 2022. | Series: The shortest history series | Includes index.
Identifiers: LCCN 2022028877 (print) | LCCN 2022028878 (ebook) | ISBN 9781615199143 (paperback) | ISBN 9781615199150 (ebook)
Subjects: LCSH: Europe--History.
Classification: LCC D102 .H567 2022 (print) | LCC D102 (ebook) | DDC 940--dc23/eng/20220616
LC record available at https://lccn.loc.gov/2022028877
LC ebook record available at https://lccn.loc.gov/2022028878

ISBN 978-1-61519-914-3
Ebook ISBN 978-1-61519-915-0

Cover and text design by Jack Dunnington

Manufactured in the United States of America

First printing November 2022
10 9 8 7 6 5 4 3 2

Contents

Introduction

I F YOU LIKE TO SKIP TO THE END OF A book to see what happens, you will enjoy this book. The endings start soon after it begins. It tells the history of Europe six times, each from a different angle.

These were originally lectures designed to introduce university students to European history. I did not start at the beginning and go through to the end. I quickly gave the students an overview and then returned later with more detail.

The first two lectures sketch out the whole of European history. This is truly the shortest history. The next six lectures take a particular theme. The aim is to deepen understanding by returning and more deeply examining.

A story has a plot: a beginning, a middle, and an end. A civilization does not have a story in this sense. We are captured by story if we think a civilization must have a rise and fall, though it will have an end. My aim here is to capture the essential elements of European civilization and to see how they have been reconfigured through time; to show how new things take their shape from old; how the old persists and returns.

History books deal with many events and people. This is one of history's strengths, and it takes us close to life. But what does it all mean? What are the really important things? These are the questions I always have in mind. Many people and events that get into other history books don't get into this one.

After classical times, the book deals chiefly with Western Europe. Not all parts of Europe are equally important in the making of European civilization. The Renaissance in Italy, the Reformation in Germany, parliamentary government in England,

and revolutionary democracy in France: These are of more consequence than the partitions of Poland.

I have relied heavily on the work of historical sociologists, particularly Michael Mann and Patricia Crone. Professor Crone is
not an expert on European history; her specialty is Islam. But in a
little book called *Pre-Industrial Societies* she included one chapter
on "The Oddity of Europe." This is a tour de force, a whole history
in thirty pages, almost as short as my shortest history. It provided
me with the concept of the making and reworking of the European mix, as set out in my first two lectures. My debt to her is
that great.

For some years at La Trobe University in Melbourne I was for-
tunate to have as a colleague Professor Eric Jones, who was a great
encourager of the big-picture approach to history and upon whose
book *The European Miracle* I have heavily relied.

I claim no originality for the book except in its method. I first
offered these lectures to students in Australia who had had too
much Australian history and knew too little of the civilization of
which they are a part.

This edition has a new section that deals in detail with the
nineteenth and twentieth centuries.

CHAPTER 1

Europe Classical and Medieval

E UROPEAN CIVILIZATION IS UNIQUE because it is the only civilization that has imposed itself on the rest of the world. It did this by conquest and settlement; by its economic power; by the power of its ideas; and because it had things that everyone else wanted. Today every country on Earth uses the discoveries of science and the technologies that flow from it, and science was a European invention.

At its beginning European civilization was made up of three elements:

1. the culture of Ancient Greece and Rome
2. Christianity, which is an odd offshoot of the religion of the Jews, Judaism
3. the culture of the German warriors who invaded the Roman Empire.

European civilization was a mixture: The importance of this will become clear as we go on.

IF WE LOOK FOR THE ORIGINS of our philosophy, our art, our literature, our math, our science, our medicine, and our thinking about politics—in all these intellectual endeavors we are taken back to Ancient Greece.

In its great days Greece was not one state; it was made up of a series of little states: city-states, as they are now called. There was a single town with a tract of land around it; everyone could walk into the town in a day. The Greeks wanted to belong to a state as we belong to a club: It was a fellowship. It was in these

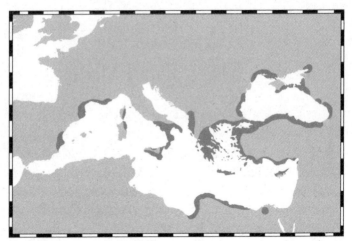

Ancient Greek cities and colonies. Greek civilization thrived in trading and agricultural colonies around the Mediterranean and Black Seas.

small city-states that the first democracies emerged. They were not representative democracies; you did not elect a member of parliament. All male citizens gathered in one place to talk about public affairs, to vote on the laws, and to vote on policy.

As these Greek city-states grew in population, they sent people to start colonies in other parts of the Mediterranean. There were Greek settlements in what is now Turkey, along the coast of North Africa, even as far west as Spain, southern France, and southern Italy. And it was there—in Italy—that the Romans, who were then a very backward people, a small city-state around Rome, first met the Greeks and began to learn from them.

In time the Romans built a huge empire that encompassed Greece and all the Greek colonies. In the north the boundaries were two great rivers, the Rhine and the Danube, though sometimes these were exceeded. In the west was the Atlantic Ocean. England was part of the Roman Empire but not Scotland or Ireland. To the south were the deserts of North Africa. In the east the boundary was most uncertain because here were rival empires. The empire encircled the Mediterranean Sea; it included only part

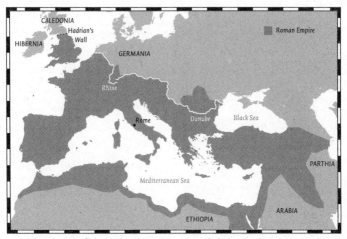

The extent of the Roman Empire around the second century AD.

of what is now Europe and much that is not Europe: Turkey, the Middle East, and North Africa.

The Romans were better than the Greeks at fighting. They were better than the Greeks at law, which they used to run their empire. They were better than the Greeks at engineering, which was useful both for fighting and running an empire. But in everything else they acknowledged that the Greeks were superior and slavishly copied them. A member of the Roman elite could speak both Greek and Latin, the language of the Romans; he sent his son to Athens for a university education or he hired a Greek slave to teach his children at home. So when we talk about the Roman Empire being Greco-Roman it is because the Romans wanted it that way.

Geometry is the quickest way to demonstrate how clever the Greeks were. The geometry taught in school is Greek. Many will have forgotten it, so let's start with the basics. That is how geometry works; it starts with a few basic definitions and builds on them. The starting point is a point, which the Greeks defined as having location but no magnitude. Of course it does possess magnitude, there is the width of the dot on the page, but geometry is a sort of make-believe world, a pure world. Second: A line has length but no breadth. Next, a straight line is defined as the shortest line joining two points. From these three definitions you can create a definition of a circle: In the first place, it is a line making a closed figure. But how do you formulate roundness? If you think about it, roundness is very hard to define. You define it by saying there is a point within this figure, one point, from which straight lines drawn to the figure will always be of equal length.

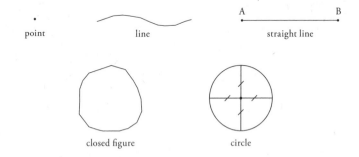

point   line   straight line

closed figure   circle

Along with circles, there are parallel lines that extend forever without meeting, and triangles in all their variety, and squares and rectangles, and other regular forms. These objects, formed by lines, are all defined, their characteristics revealed, and the possibilities arising from their intersection and overlapping explored. Everything is proved from what has been established before. For example, by using a quality of parallel lines, you can show that the angles of a triangle add up to 180 degrees (see box, page 7).

Geometry is a simple, elegant, logical system, very satisfying, and beautiful. Beautiful? The Greeks found it beautiful and that they did so is a clue to the Greek mind. The Greeks did geometry not just as an exercise, which is why we did it at school, nor for its practical uses in surveying or navigation. They saw geometry as a guide to the fundamental nature of the universe. When we look around us, we are struck by the variety of what we see: different shapes, different colors. A whole range of things is happening

Geometry in action

Parallel lines do not meet. We can define this characteristic by saying that a line drawn across them will create alternate angles that are equal. If they were not equal, the lines would come together or they would diverge—they would not be parallel. We use letters from the Greek alphabet to identify an angle—and on the diagram on the left α marks two angles that are equal. The use of letters from the Greek alphabet for the signage in geometry reminds us of its origins. Here we use the first three letters: alpha, beta, and gamma.

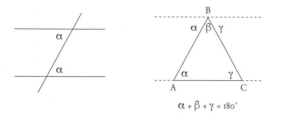

$$\alpha + \beta + \gamma = 180°$$

From this definition we can determine the sum of the angles within a triangle. We put the triangle ABC on the right within two parallel lines: Knowing how to bring into play what is known to solve what is unknown is the trick of geometry. The angle α at point A has an angle that is equal to it at point B, on the basis that they are alternate angles across parallel lines. Likewise the angle γ at C has an angle equal to it at point B. The top parallel line at B is now made up of three angles: α + β + γ. Together they make a straight line, and we know that straight lines make an angle of 180 degrees.

So α + β + γ = 180 degrees. And we have established, using parallel lines, that the sum of the internal angles of the triangle is also α + β + γ. So the sum of the internal angles of a triangle is 180 degrees.

We have used parallel lines to prove something about triangles.

simultaneously—randomly, chaotically. The Greeks believed there was some simple explanation for all this. That underneath all this variety there must be something simple, regular, and logical that explains it all. Something like geometry.

The Greeks did not do science as we do, with hypotheses and testing by experiment. They thought if you got your mind into gear and thought hard you would get the right answer. So they proceeded by a system of inspired guesses. One Greek philosopher said all matter is made up of water, which shows how desperate they were to get a simple answer. Another philosopher said all matter is made up of four things: earth, fire, air, and water. Another philosopher said all matter is actually made up of little things that he called atoms—and hit the jackpot. He made an inspired guess which we came back to in the twentieth century.

When science as we know it began 400 years ago, 2,000 years after the Greeks, it began by upsetting the central teachings of Greek science, which remained the authority. But it upset the Greeks by following this Greek hunch that the answers would be simple and logical and mathematical. Newton, the great seventeenth-century scientist, and Einstein, the great twentieth-century scientist, both said you will only get close to a correct answer if your answer is simple. They were both able to give their answers in mathematical equations that described the composition of matter and how matter moves.

The Greeks were often wrong in their guesses, very wrong. Their fundamental hunch that the answers would be simple, mathematical, and logical could have been wrong too, but it turned out to be right. This is the greatest legacy that European civilization still owes to the Greeks.

Can we explain why the Greeks were so clever? I don't think we can. Historians are meant to be able to explain things but when they come up against the big things—why, for example, in these little city-states there were minds so logical, so agile, and so penetrating—they have no convincing explanation. All historians can do, like anyone else, is wonder.

Here is another miracle. We are coming to the second element in the European mix. The Jews came to believe that there was only one god. This was a very unusual view. The Greeks and Romans had the more common belief that there were many gods. The Jews had an even more extraordinary belief that this one god took special care of them; that they were God's chosen people. In return, the Jews had to keep God's law. The foundation of the law was the Ten Commandments, given to the Jews by Moses, who had led them out of captivity in Egypt. Christians retained the Ten Commandments and they remained the central moral teaching in the West until recent times. People knew the commandments by number. You might say of someone that he would never break the eighth commandment, but sometimes he broke the seventh. Here are the Ten Commandments, as recorded in the second book of the Bible, Exodus, Chapter 20.

And God spoke all these words, saying, I am the Lord your God, who brought you out of the land of Egypt, out of the house of bondage.

You shall have no other gods before me.

You shall not make for yourself a carved image, or any likeness of anything that is in heaven above, or that is in the earth beneath, or that is in the water under the earth.

You shall not take the name of the Lord your God in vain, for the Lord will not hold him guiltless who takes his name in vain.

Remember the sabbath day, to keep it holy. Six days you shall labor and do all your work, for in six days the Lord made the heavens and the earth, the sea, and all that is in them, and rested the seventh day. Therefore the Lord blessed the sabbath day and hallowed it.

Honor your father and your mother, that your days may be long upon the land which the Lord your God is giving to you.

You shall not kill.

You shall not commit adultery.

You shall not steal.

You shall not bear false witness against your neighbor.

You shall not desire for yourself your neighbor's house, your neighbor's wife, nor his male servant, nor his female servant, nor his ox, nor his donkey, nor anything that is your neighbor's.

The Ten Commandments were only the beginning of the moral law. The Jews had a very complex, detailed system of law that covers the matters law usually does—crime, property, inheritance, and marriage—but also diet, cleanliness, the running of a household, and how to make sacrifices to God at the temple.

Though the Jews believed they were the chosen people, they didn't have a dream run. They were frequently humiliated; they were conquered and taken into exile; but they didn't doubt that God existed or that he cared for them. If disaster struck they concluded that they had not been following the law properly, that they had offended God. So in the religion of the Jews, as in Christianity, religion and morality are closely linked, which is not the case with all religions. The Romans and Greeks had gods who acted immorally, who had affairs and plotted against each other. In the Roman religion the gods might punish, but usually not for any moral offense; it might be that you hadn't sacrificed correctly, or often enough.

Jesus, the founder of Christianity, was a Jew, and his first followers were all Jews. When Jesus taught, the Jews were again not in control of their country; Palestine was a distant province of the Roman Empire. Some of the followers of Jesus looked to him to lead a revolt against Rome. His opponents tried to trick him into a declaration to this effect. Should we pay taxes to Rome, they asked him. Hand me a coin, he said—whose image is on it? Caesar's, they replied. Jesus said, "Give to Caesar what is Caesar's and to God what is God's."

Jesus knew the Jewish law and teaching very well and his own teaching grew out of this. Part of his teaching was to sum up the essence of the law. This was one of his summations: Love the Lord your God with all your heart, with all your soul, with all your mind, and love your neighbor as yourself.

It is not clear whether Jesus was saying you can take the summary and forget all the detail. Or whether he was saying that the detail is important—about cleanliness, sacrifice, and all the rest—but the summary is a guide to the most important things.

Scholars argue about how far Jesus remained within Judaism or was breaking out of it. But one thing is clear: He extended the old moral teaching in ways which were very demanding and which you might think impossible to follow. Just consider what he said about loving your enemies in the Sermon on the Mount, as recorded in Matthew's Gospel, Chapter 5:

> Our forefathers were told, love your neighbor, hate your enemy. But what I tell you is this: Love your enemies and pray for your persecutors. Only so can you be children of your Heavenly Father, who makes his sun rise on good and on bad alike and sends the rain on the honest and on the dishonest. If you love only those who love you, what reward can you expect? Surely the tax-gatherers [the hated Roman tax-gatherers] do as much as that. And if you greet only your brothers, what is there extraordinary about that? Even the heathen do as much. You must therefore be all goodness. Just as your Heavenly Father is all good.

On this occasion, Jesus was transforming the Jewish code into a system of universal love.

Jesus was only one of many teachers and prophets at this time. They aroused the suspicion of the leaders of the Jewish faith, and in Jesus's case the leaders of the Jews co-operated with the Romans in having Jesus executed. But Jesus was different from these other teachers because after he was dead he came alive again—or so his followers believed. So he was not just a teacher, a prophet, or a good man, which is probably the belief of many church-going people today. His followers believed that he was God's son and that something of cosmic significance had happened when Jesus was crucified. God had sacrificed himself to save human-kind from damnation, a consequence of man's original sin that brought evil into the world. If you believed in Christ you could save yourself and after death you would not be condemned to hellfire but you would be forever with God in heaven.

Was this religion just for the Jews or was it for everyone? Jesus's followers after his death were divided on this question. The traditionalists said that you could only become a Christian if you became a Jew first and so followed all the strict rules that were laid down for the Jews in the Old Testament. That would have included circumcision, which for adult males is a rather painful operation. If this path had been taken, Christianity would have remained a very small sect of the Jewish faith and probably have died out or certainly been of no great significance. The other side won, the side that said, this is a totally new religion. You don't have to become a Jew first; all the restrictions of the law can go; Christ has set us free from all that; his teaching about love surpasses anything that the law could offer. This is the view of Paul, the great early missionary of the church and, according to some, the founder of Christianity, because when Jesus died this faith was a Jewish affair only. Jesus was a Jew, and his followers were Jews, some of whom wanted to keep it that way. It was Paul who most clearly said this is a religion for everyone and so from that time Christianity became, potentially at least, a world religion. Within 300 years it had spread right throughout the Roman Empire.

The third group in the mixture are the German warriors who invaded the Roman Empire. They lived on the northern borders and in the 400s they flooded in. By AD 476 they had destroyed the empire in the west. It was here in France, Spain, and Italy that the mixture of European civilization first took shape.

The Germans were illiterate and left no written records, and so we have very little information about them before they invaded. The best account—probably not a firsthand account—is by a Roman historian, Tacitus, in the first century AD. He describes the chiefs and companions who lived and fought together and who lived for fighting:

On the field of battle, it is a disgrace for the chief to be outdone in courage by his companions, and for the companions not to equal the courage of their chief. As for leaving a battle alive after your chief has fallen, that means lifelong infamy and shame. To defend and protect him, to put down one's own acts of heroism to his credit; that is what they really mean by allegiance. The chiefs fight for victory, the companions for their chief. Many noble youths, if the land of their birth is stagnating in a long peace, deliberately seek out other tribes where some war is afoot. The Germans have no taste for peace. Fame is easier won among perils and you cannot maintain a large body of companions except by violence and war. The companions are always asking things of their chiefs: Give me that warhorse or give me that bloody and victorious spear. As for meals, with their plentiful if homely fare, they count simply as pay. Such openhandedness must have war and plunder to feed it. You will find it harder to persuade a German to plow the land and to await its annual produce with patience than to challenge a foe and to earn the prize of wounds. He thinks it is spiritless and base to gain by sweat what he can buy with blood.

These are the people who, 300 years later, took over the Roman Empire.

We have now examined the three elements. Let us summarize them. The Greek view was that *the world is simple, logical, and mathematical*. The Christian view was that *the world is evil, and Christ alone saves*. The German warriors' view was that *fighting is fun*. It is this unlikely mixture that comes together to make European civilization.

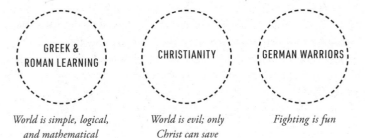

GREEK & ROMAN LEARNING

CHRISTIANITY

GERMAN WARRIORS

World is simple, logical, and mathematical

World is evil; only Christ can save

Fighting is fun

How were the three elements brought together? First, consider Christianity's connection with the Greco-Roman world. The Roman authorities from time to time tried to stamp out Christianity. They seized the holy books; they confiscated church property; they arrested and tortured Christians; they executed those who wouldn't deny Christ.

The Romans were usually very tolerant. They ruled an empire that was composed of a variety of races and religions; if you kept the peace the Romans were prepared to let you follow your own path. You could govern yourself. You could practice your own religion, with this exception: You had to sacrifice to the emperor. The Romans believed the emperor was something like a god. The sacrifice you were required to make was trifling. There might be a portrait or statue of the emperor and, in front of it, a flame. You had to take a pinch of salt and drop it in the flame. The flame would flare up. That was enough. It was like saluting the flag or singing the national anthem. The Christians wouldn't do it because, like the Jews, they said they must worship only one god and they would not treat the emperor as in any way a god. The Romans usually excused the Jews from honoring the emperor. They thought of them as cranky and volatile, but recognizable, an ancient people with their temple and their god, occupying a certain tract of country. By contrast, Christians were following a new religion and Christians could be anyone, anywhere. The Romans thought of them as subversives who had to be eliminated. They might have succeeded in this if they had consistently maintained the persecution.

Then a miracle happened. An emperor, Constantine, in AD 313 became a Christian or at least gave official support to the Christian churches. He thought their god might look after him and the empire better than any other. When Christianity was still far from being a majority faith, the ruler of the state embraced it; he gave the churches money and endorsed the rule of the bishops. Fifty years later, another Christian emperor outlawed all other religions. Four hundred years after Jesus taught in a troubled and distant province of the Roman Empire, Christianity became the official and sole religion of the empire. The bishops and priests now paraded around the towns and marched into the countryside to destroy the pagan temples. This is the first link among the three elements: *The Roman Empire becomes Christian.*

By this stage the church was very different from what it had been in its early days. At

Constantine (272–337), the Roman emperor who gave official support to Christianity in AD 313.

first, groups of Christians had met in private houses. Now, three or four centuries later, there was a complete hierarchy of full-time paid officials: priests, bishops, and archbishops. One of the bishops—the bishop of Rome—had managed to make himself into the pope and to govern the church. The church had its own system of law and its own courts and jails to enforce its law. The church governed quite important matters like marriage and inheritance, not just church affairs. The church ran and enforced its own system of taxation because everyone was obliged to pay money to support it.

When the Roman Empire collapsed, the church survived—it was like a government in itself. The pope was a parallel figure to the Roman emperor, controlling a hierarchy of officials beneath him. Here we see the second link in the making of the mixture: *The church becomes Roman.*

After the Roman Empire collapsed, the church preserved the learning of Greece and Rome (which it had already begun to do). This is an amazing development because all the writers, philosophers, and scientists of ancient Greece and Rome were pagan, not Christian. Why would the Christian church bother with such people? There was one group in the Christian church who said that they should not, that their writings were falsehoods and the only truth is in Christ. "What has Athens to do with Jerusalem?" said Tertullian. But that view did not prevail.

The Christians did not set up their own system of education, so when Christianity began to order and systematize its beliefs it relied on educated people who were steeped in the Greco-Roman tradition. They used Greek philosophy and Greek logic to explain and defend Christianity. These Christian scholars thought of the great philosophers and moralists of Greece and Rome as possessing some of the truth, though Christianity was of course the full truth. But the Greek philosophers could be used as a guide to the truth and to argue about the truth. So although they were pagan, the church preserved and used their writings. This is the third link: *The church preserves Greek and Roman learning.*

When the Germans invaded the Roman Empire, they did not intend to destroy it. They were coming for plunder, to get the best lands, and to settle down and enjoy the good things in life. They were happy to acknowledge the emperor's rule. But the trouble was that in the 400s so many Germans came and took so much land, there was nothing left for the emperor to control. In effect, the Roman Empire came to an end because there was nothing left to rule.

For their part the German warriors found that they had to run the societies they had invaded, which is not really what they expected to do, and they had to do so in very difficult circumstances. They themselves were illiterate; in the chaos that they had caused, the remaining Roman administration collapsed; trade and the towns shrank. The warrior chiefs set themselves up as kings and created little kingdoms; they fought among themselves; kingdoms rose and fell rapidly. It was many centuries before the outlines of the modern states of Western Europe appeared: France, Spain, England.

Governments in these circumstances were extremely weak. They were so weak they were not able even to collect taxation. (To us this seems like a contradiction in terms—a government that doesn't tax!) Instead of being the chief, the German warrior now turned himself into a king and allotted land to his companions, who were turning themselves into the nobility, on the condition that when the king needed an army the nobles would provide it for him. They would send so many soldiers. But the nobles began to treat the land as if it were their own and to have their own views about how many soldiers they would send, and of what quality and for what purpose.

Today, heads of state inspect guards of honor. They move along the ranks, appearing to scrutinize the soldiers, perhaps saying a word or two. This is a carryover from an early medieval practice when the king was really scrutinizing the soldiers he had been sent and saying to himself: What sort of garbage have they sent this time?

There was a long fight for kings to get more power: to be able to rule without being in the hands of the nobles; to get their own system of taxation; to have an army that they fully controlled; to get their own bureaucracy. But because they started from such a weak position, there were some things that they were never able to threaten. Private property became sacrosanct; the nobles had turned land held on condition into private property. This always put a limitation on governments, so that though the powers of European kings grew they never became like Eastern rulers, who owned everything in their realm. If a despot was in need of assets he would simply seize someone's property or send his troops down to the bazaar to grab a pile of merchandise. European governments, even when called "absolute," could never act like that. *Not everything is the king's* was the foundation of European thinking about government. From the right to private property derives the notion of individual rights, which is a central part of the Western tradition. The notion that government must be limited arose because, at the beginning, government, in fact, was extremely limited.

This limitation on government was also important for economic development. The security that merchants enjoyed was an important reason why it was in Europe that economic growth took off in a way not matched anywhere else.

Knowing what we do about these warriors and their attitude, we should not be surprised that soon after invading the empire, they became Christian. The church was the only institution that survived the collapse of the Roman Empire. It was often the bishop who went out to negotiate with the warrior band as it arrived bent on plunder. It was the bishop who said: "You can have the land on that side of the river, but please leave the rest to us." He might point out the palace of the former Roman governor, which the chief would no doubt claim for himself, and suggest that he would visit him there soon to help in running the place. Quite quickly the bishops were able to persuade the warriors that they would kill more of their enemies if they accepted the Christian god. These were conquerors of a special sort: They accepted the religion of the people they had conquered. The church made it quite clear to these new rulers, kings, and nobles, that one of their duties was to uphold the Christian faith. This is our last link: *German warriors support Christianity.*

If we summarize all the links:

ROMAN EMPIRE *becomes* CHRISTIAN
CHRISTIAN CHURCH *becomes* ROMAN
CHURCH *preserves* GREEK & ROMAN LEARNING
GERMAN WARRIORS *become* CHRISTIAN

we reach this conclusion:

It is a very odd mixture, isn't it? These are not natural allies. It is an unstable mixture. Eventually it will break open, but it held together for about a thousand years—from around AD 476, the date of the fall of the Roman Empire, to about 1400. This is the period historians call the Middle Ages or the medieval period. Historians who take a large view of things regard 1400 as the beginning of modern times. Here are the three eras of European history: ancient or classical; medieval; modern.

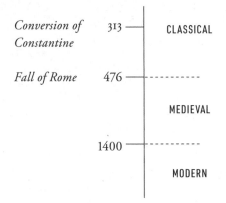

Throughout the Middle Ages this odd trio holds together, but the elements do change. Consider Christianity. Whatever else it was, it wasn't a warlike religion. Jesus said: "Love your enemies." The early Christians refused military service, one reason the Romans were suspicious of them. But now the Christians are in partnership with German warriors. This turn-the-other-cheek religion is supported by iron men. What sort of contradiction is this? It is not as great as it seems, because once Christianity had been taken up by Constantine and become an official state religion it had to change its views about violence. Governments must fight, and if the church wanted the support of governments it had to agree that governments can sometimes fight justly.

Yet, when the church teamed up with these warriors it did not fully accept their values. Over the centuries, the warrior changed into the knight. A knight loved fighting, was proud of his ability to fight, but fought for good causes. The church encouraged him to fight non-Christians— that was a very good cause indeed. The church promoted the crusades to the Holy Land, which had fallen into Muslim hands. Special dispensation was offered if you went and fought there.

A knight also protected the weak, especially highborn women. So with this new moral overtone to his fighting, a man became a knight in a sort of

King Charles of the Franks (Charlemagne) buckles a sword onto Roland who, according to legend, died fighting the Muslims in Spain.

religious ceremony. His sword was placed on the altar in a Christian church and then buckled onto the knight, who would then go off and do good things with it.

This attitude of protecting and honoring ladies was long-lasting in European culture. After the knights disappeared it became the attitude of a "gentleman," the descendant of the Christian knight. A gentleman showed respect for women by standing when women came into the room, by refusing to be seated while women were standing, and by tipping his hat to women. I was taught this at school and find it hard to forget. In this, I'm a living relic of the Middle Ages.

Feminists in recent times fought against this respect. They did not want to be honored on a pedestal; they wanted to be equal. In their campaign for equality they had the advantage of height; better to start on a pedestal than ground firmly underfoot. It was because women had this degree of respect in European culture that feminism was fairly readily accepted. It is a different story in other cultures.

Let us look at another tension in this mix: the Christian church's preservation of Greek and Roman learning. This was an active process of preservation; it wasn't as if the church merely put the clever books in a cupboard and left them there. They have only survived—and we can only read them now—because the church copied and recopied them right through the Middle Ages. There was no printing; books rot and perish. It was the monks in the monasteries, often not knowing what they were copying—hence the many mistakes—who preserved so much of the treasures of Greece and Rome.

If read in its own terms, this literature presents a philosophy, a system of values, an attitude to life which is un-Christian, pagan. But the church in the Middle Ages was able to maintain such command over intellectual life that no one ever looked at this literature in its own terms. Instead, the church borrowed what it wanted, reassembled the parts it had taken, put them with passages from the Bible, and so constructed a Christian theology, that is, an account of God and God's world and his plan of sal-

vation. So Greek philosophy, Greek learning, and Greek logic were all pressed into service in support of Christianity. New discoveries of ancient texts did not disturb the scholars; they wove new discoveries into a new version of their theology.

Let us summarize how the mix was working in the Middle Ages. We have *warriors becoming Christian knights*, we have *Greek and Roman*

The Christian church preserved Greek and Roman learning and used it to support its own doctrine.

learning supporting Christianity. The church, in the middle of this odd alliance, is managing to hold the whole thing together. Learning is Christian, the knights are Christian, the world is *Christendom*, the realm of Christ.

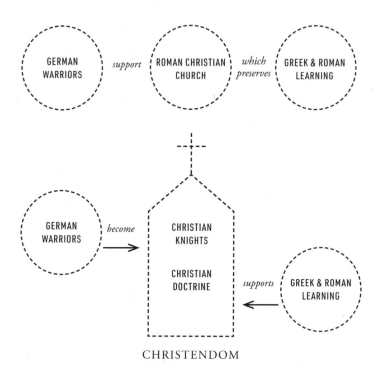

CHRISTENDOM

After the year 1400, this strange alliance begins to break apart and what historians call modern times begin.

CHAPTER 2

Europe Modern

THE MIXTURE THAT FORMED European civilization was an unstable one. It lasted for a long time—through the Middle Ages, a thousand years—but its elements were not in harmony with each other. Around the year 1400, the mixture began to come apart. This occurred first in the Renaissance.

The Renaissance is often depicted as the discovery or rediscovery of Greek and Roman learning. But it wasn't so much that the learning had been lost and had to be rediscovered, though some new discoveries were made at this time. What had changed was that instead of the church's using ancient learning to support its theology, now there were scholars, chiefly outside the church, who were interested in imagining the Greek and Roman world as it existed when the learning was produced. They wanted to make art like the ancient artists did, to build buildings like theirs, to write Latin like they did, to think like they did. They were thinking themselves back into a previous world that was un-Christian and pagan—something that the church had hidden as it had used this learning for its own purposes.

It was also a more "worldly" world. The ancients had been far more concerned with men and their doings on this earth than with their life after death. The ancients had celebrated man's capacity and powers and they hadn't dwelt on his depravity. It was a very open-minded world that the Renaissance scholars now entered. There was a huge variety of views among the ancient philosophers and moralists on how best to live and what best to think. Their debates and speculations had not been carried on within the sort of straitjacket that the church had imposed on thinking.

However, the scholars of the Renaissance did not directly attack Christianity. They varied in their individual attitudes, but broadly they took a view of the Christian religion that was similar to the ancients' own view of religion. That is, religion was something unproblematically present, it was broadly a good thing or a necessary thing, but there were many other things to be interested in. Religion was not to control all of life and thought, which had been the church's aim. Once that control had been broken, European thought became much more adventurous, more broad-minded, and less given to certainty than it had been previously.

With the Renaissance begins the long process of the secularization of European society. A secular world is one in which religion might exist, but it exists as a private business or as an association of people who are attached to certain beliefs—as in our world. Religion doesn't dominate society; it does not impose its rules and rituals on everyone, or control thought.

What happened in the Renaissance was that the people of one culture and tradition thought themselves into another culture and tradition. Once you've done that, you are never the same again. Nothing ever seems as certain and fixed. Not for the last time, European thinkers had jumped out of their own skin.

The men of the Renaissance were the first to call the age of Greece and Rome the classical era. Classic here means the very best: a classic catch, a classic performance, something that cannot be surpassed. They believed that the achievements of the ancients in literature, art, philosophy, and science were unsurpassed and unsurpassable. They themselves would do well if they could come close to equaling it. So the Renaissance disrupted the mixture with the message: *the classics are supreme*.

Our system of time works on two different bases, which is a constant reminder of the mixed nature of our civilization. We date years from the birth of Christ and in that sense we still acknowledge ourselves as a Christian civilization. AD is an abbreviation of the Latin *Anno Domini*, "in the year of the Lord" (who was actually

GERMAN WARRIORS — *support* → ROMAN CHRISTIAN CHURCH — *which preserves* → GREEK & ROMAN LEARNING

↓

C15 RENAISSANCE
Classics are supreme

born not in the year I AD but more likely 6 or 4 BC). However, the way we divide time into eras—classical, medieval, and modern—has nothing to do with Christianity. It is the Renaissance view, which says that the classical world reached a peak of perfection and then mankind wandered and lost touch with its heritage. This period of "time-out" is the so-called Middle Ages, which is the very time when the church reached its preeminence in intellectual and social life. So classical, medieval, modern is a very un-Christian formulation.

Three sculptures can illustrate the threefold movement of classical, medieval, and modern. The first is an ancient Greek sculpture, which is why one of the arms no longer survives. Not many of the original Greek sculptures survive; what we have are usually Roman copies, which are not nearly as good. This is the god Hermes with the infant Dionysus by Praxiteles. The human body as a thing of beauty and perfection is a Greek invention. As the art historian Kenneth Clark says, the nude is to be distinguished from the naked body. The nude is sufficient in itself, very properly in this state; the naked body is without clothes and reduced by their absence. Of course, most male bodies don't look like this: The aim of the Greeks was not to represent a particular body. They worked to find perfection in the body and they used their mathematics to establish the proportions that are most pleasing and beautiful.

Hermes by Praxiteles

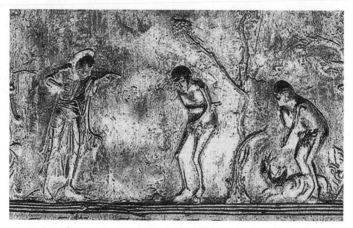
God confronts Adam and Eve, from the bronze doors at Hildesheim

The second sculpture is a medieval view of the human form; these figures are on the cathedral doors at Hildesheim in Germany. This is Adam and Eve after they have eaten the fruit that God said they should not eat. Adam is blaming Eve; Eve is blaming the serpent; both are ashamed of their nakedness, which in part they cover. These are very definitely not nudes; they embody the Christian teaching that the body is evil, a source of sin.

The third is Michelangelo in the Renaissance, modeling himself on the Greeks and returning to their idea of the nude. He renders his David as a human form of perfection: man as the embodiment of something high-spirited, noble, and beautiful—as Hamlet says, "in action how like an angel, in apprehension how like a god."

From nude to naked to nude can stand for the movement from classical to medieval to modern, which is how the Renaissance understood itself.

David by Michelangelo

THE RENAISSANCE WAS THE first great disruption of the medieval world; the second was the Protestant Reformation of the sixteenth century. This was a direct attack on the church. Its aim was to return the Christian church to what it was like before it became Roman. As we have seen, the church acquired its Roman features because it grew up within the Roman Empire; when the empire collapsed, the church continued with its pope, who was like an emperor figure, and archbishops and bishops, who were like the administrators of the old Roman Empire, and beneath them in every locality the priests. This holy body had its laws, its punishments, its jails, and its system of taxation.

The pope and the bishops ruled the church and determined its teaching. The church offered you salvation but only by means that it controlled. You needed priests and bishops in order to be saved. You had to take the communion, the mass, and you needed a priest to create the magic of turning the bread and the wine into the body and blood of Jesus. You needed a priest to hear your confession, to grant forgiveness, and set the penance for your sins. The priest might instruct you to say so many Hail Marys or to go on a pilgrimage or, for a severe offense, to allow yourself to be whipped before the altar. If you were rich and dying, the priest might tell you very firmly that you would not go to heaven unless you left a good deal of your wealth to the church.

In the Middle Ages, most priests, bishops, and archbishops did not enter the church because they were particularly pious or religious; men joined the church because it was the largest and richest organization of the day. You took holy orders for the same reasons as today you would go into the civil service or a large corporation or politics or to a university: to get a secure job, to get interesting work, to get a high salary, to live well, and to exercise power. In the church there was plenty of opportunity for enriching yourself and giving jobs to friends and relatives.

Yet this rich, plundering, corrupt organization was also the preserver of the teachings of Jesus and the accounts of the early

Christians. Jesus and his followers had been humble people but now popes and bishops lived in palaces. Jesus had warned against the dangers of riches, and the early Christians had simply met in each other's houses. All this is recorded in the Bible, so the church's holy document could be dynamite in the hands of its critics. How did the church manage to escape for so long from a devastating critique?

As the Bible was in Latin, very few people could read it. The church said it was the first and final authority for interpreting the Bible. If anyone used the Bible to criticize the teaching or the practice of the church and made a real nuisance of themselves, they were burned as heretics—that is, as false believers, a danger to themselves and to Christendom. But then in the sixteenth century, with the Reformation, there was a heretic who got away. His name was Martin Luther.

Luther was a monk who took his religion very seriously. He agonized over his own salvation: What could he do, he who was so sinful, to be saved? Then his mind was suddenly put at rest while reading in the Bible Paul's letter to the church in Rome. Here Paul says your faith in Christ will save you. From this, Luther deduced that you didn't have to *do* anything to be saved,

in particular, you didn't have to put yourself in the hands of the priests and follow their instructions. All you had to do was to believe, to have faith; *faith alone will save you* is the central Lutheran message. Believe in Christ and you will be saved. Now as a believer, of course, you will want to do things to please God, to do, as the church says, good works, to act as Christ says we should

Martin Luther by Lucas Cranach, 1532.

act. But those works in themselves will not help you to be saved. This is where Protestant and Catholic teaching differed fundamentally. The Catholics emphasized good works as part of the process of salvation. Going on a pilgrimage, giving your money to the poor: That will help your cause with God. Luther said it will not—how could anything we do, we who are so sinful and corrupt, make us pleasing in God's eyes? The only thing we can do is to believe, and if we believe, God has promised that we will be saved.

This is a sort of do-it-yourself religion; all that huge apparatus that the church had built up over the centuries, Luther said, was unnecessary. This view did not go down well in Rome. The pope rejected Luther's criticisms of the church and his new teaching about salvation. Luther replied with fierce denunciations of the pope. *Who does this man think he is? He is the representative of Christ on earth, so we are told, yet he is really the enemy of Christ, the anti-Christ. He lives in pomp, wears a triple crown, when you come into his presence you have to kiss his toe, when he moves he is carried shoulder-high by his servants—and yet we know from the Bible that Christ went around on foot.* The Bible: That was the key to Luther's criticism of the church. If something was not in the Bible, the church was not justified in insisting on it or practicing it. The Bible was the sole authority. After his break with Rome, the first thing Luther did was to translate the Bible into German so everyone could read it and become the managers of their own salvation.

The Protestant Reformation was the movement to reform the church by basing teaching and practice on the Bible. It wanted to recover the life of the early church. The message of the Reformation was *Christianity is not Roman.*

How did Luther escape being burned as a heretic? There are a number of reasons. One was the invention of printing. All Luther's criticisms and denunciations of the church were immediately put into print and circulated widely through Europe.

Printing was a new invention, only fifty years old when Luther began his attack on the church. Before the pope could organize to defeat Luther, everyone knew of him, everyone was reading his criticisms. This was not a heretic with just a few followers in one country, as there had been many times before; this man very quickly had an international following. The other reason Luther survived is that some of the German princes welcomed his attack on Rome. Germany was not one country; it was a collection of many states. Partly because of this the church exercised more influence in Germany than in the unified countries of France and England. It held an immense amount of land, almost half in some places, collected large sums of money from the people, and the pope appointed bishops without the princes' having a say. By following Luther, the princes were able to seize the church lands, appoint their own bishops, and stop the flow of money to Rome. The princes became the protectors of Luther, and in their realms the Lutheran church began. The Lutheran church was established in about half of Germany, and from Germany Lutheranism spread north into Sweden, Denmark, and Norway. England adopted its own brand of Protestantism, the Church of England.

Quite quickly there was more than one rival of the church of Rome. The Protestant churches took a number of forms, a different one in each country. They were self-sufficient within their countries, a series of national churches, whereas the Catholic church was an international organization. Once people began to read the Bible for themselves, as Luther and the other reformers encouraged them to do, they soon found reasons in it to criticize Luther too. The Protestant movement kept spinning off new churches because there was no longer a central authority to interpret the Bible and to police belief.

For over a hundred years, Catholics and Protestants fought each other, literally fought each other, in wars. Each regarded the other as totally wrong, not as a different sort of Christian, not even as non-Christian, but rather as anti-Christian, as the enemy of the true church. The true church could only be preserved if the other side was eliminated, and that murderous doctrine led to slaughter. It was better that a Catholic or a Protestant be killed than that they preach a doctrine that was absolutely offensive to God and damaging to his church on Earth. Yet after fighting each other for a hundred years and neither side winning, the two sides arrived at a sort of long truce, and gradually the notion of toleration arose. First, it was accepted that there can be Protestant countries and Catholic countries, and then—a big jump—that perhaps different sorts of Christians can live peacefully in one country, something neither Protestants nor Catholics believed at first.

The Renaissance and the Reformation were both backward-looking movements; they were trying to separate one part of the founding mixture from the rest. The Renaissance was looking backward to Greek and Roman learning. The Protestant reformers were looking backward to the Christian church before it assumed its Roman structure. The Catholic church had harbored the documents that were central to both movements. It had preserved Greek and Roman learning, which the Renaissance used to escape its intellectual authority, and it had created and sanctified the Bible, which the Protestant reformers used to disrupt its theology and unity.

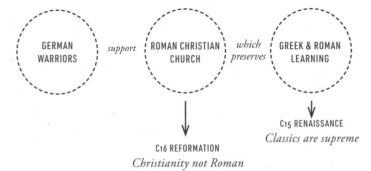

WE NOW HAVE TO LOOK AT the process by which European culture became forward-looking; how it came to believe in progress, that things over time will get better, which is a very odd thing to believe. The belief in progress came about as a result of the Scientific Revolution of the seventeenth century. This is the period when our modern science begins.

At the beginning of the seventeenth century, the Greeks were still the authority on the universe and how it worked. Their central teaching was that the Earth is at the center of the universe and around the Earth go all the other planets, including the moon and the sun. The Earth, according to the Greeks, was still; it did not appear to move—what force could possibly move it? It is stationary. The Earth is the impure realm; on Earth things change and decay, but the heavens are a pure, perfect, and unchanging realm. Why do the planets go in circles? Because the circle is a perfect form. It is one of the teachings of Greek geometry that there are perfect forms: The square is one, the circle is another. So the planets go in circles and because this is the perfect realm; they do not need any force to move them. They are spinning in perfect circular harmony.

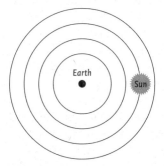

In the seventeenth century, that view was overthrown by what we still regard as the truth. The sun is at the center of the system; the planets go around the sun, not in circles but in ellipses; the Earth is one of the planets going around the sun, and around the

Earth goes the moon. The system is a single system; gone are the separate realms, impure Earth and pure heavens. It is one system throughout, and one law or one series of laws explains the whole thing.

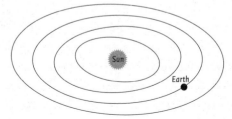

What makes the Earth and the planets move? The answer, said Isaac Newton, is that everything in the universe will continue to move in a straight line unless something else acts on it. A something else that is always present is the attraction between every body that exists in the universe. All bodies are attracting each other: This book is being attracted to the Earth, the moon is attracted to the Earth, the Earth is attracted to the sun. The water on the Earth is pulled up and down in tides because of the changing force of attraction between Earth and moon. It is the one system that holds all matter together. We can now determine why the planets move as they do. There are two forces acting on them: the tendency to move in a straight line and the tendency to be attracted to the sun. The result of the two tendencies is that the planet is tipped into its elliptical course around the sun.

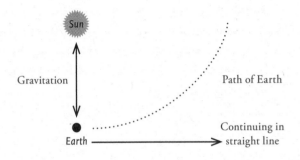

To this attraction between all bodies, Newton gave the term "gravitation," and he was able to work out the force of the gravitation between any two bodies with his Universal Law of Gravitation. The law is expressed as a mathematical formula. It says the force of gravitation will grow stronger as the bodies get bigger: It will relate directly to their mass. The force of attraction will become weaker as the distance between the bodies increases: It relates in inverse proportion to the distance between them. So the attraction increases as the mass of the two bodies gets larger, and it decreases as they get further apart. In fact, it decreases very rapidly as the bodies move apart; the force of attraction weakens by the distance between the two bodies squared. So a doubling of the distance makes the force four times as weak (2 x 2). Here is the formula, the only equation I will trouble you with. Newton used it to measure the attraction between the Earth and the sun.

$$F = G \, \frac{m_1 \times m_2}{r^2}$$

where:
- F is the magnitude of the gravitational force between the two bodies
- G is the gravitational constant
- m_1 is the mass of the first body
- m_2 is the mass of the second body
- r is the distance between the two bodies

An equation like this reminds us that math is at the center of science and that the Greek hunch turned out to be true: The world is simple and the laws governing it will be mathematical in form. The scientists of the seventeenth century overturned Greek learning on the universe but they did so with the Greek method of mathematics.

What a magnificent achievement it was to find out from where we are—on Earth, which is the third planet from the sun—how the whole system works! How natural it was for humans to put themselves at the center of the universe. How natural to follow the evidence of their senses and assume that the Earth was still. How proper to respect the learning of the magnificent Greeks. Against all these tendencies, science in the seventeenth century had its triumph.

The message of the Scientific Revolution was *the Greeks were wrong*. The great reverence for the classics was broken. We have done better than equal them; we have surpassed them.

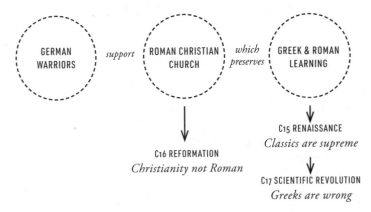

How clever these scientists were, but where had their cleverness gotten them? They had discovered that humans were marginal, that they were not at the center of the universe. This is a common Western predicament; we are very clever but we keep discovering we are insignificant. Worse was to come in the nineteenth century when Darwin advanced the view that we share a common ancestor with the apes. This was a further demoting of man and his presumption. We are not at the center of the universe, we are not a special creation, we are descended from the animal kingdom by a system of chance happenings.

The church, in both its Protestant and Catholic forms, opposed the new teaching that the sun was at the center of the universe and the Earth revolved around it. God made the Earth, said the Bible, and then set the sun and moon and stars above it. Eventually the church had to give way and declare that the scientists were right—as it did again after first contesting Darwin, with a great loss of authority on both occasions.

The generation after the Scientific Revolution did not consider that its discoveries had reduced the significance of man. On the contrary, they thought if we can do this—if by our reason we have worked out how the whole system operates and described it exactly with our math—then we can use our reason to go further; we can bring that reason to bear on human life and improve it out of all recognition. This desire to make reason sovereign is what animated the Enlightenment, an intellectual movement of the eighteenth century that aimed to apply reason to the reshaping of society, to government, to morality, and to theology.

The Enlightenment began and was strongest in France. The scholars of the Enlightenment saw the world as governed by ignorance and superstition. The two great irrational forces in the society were the church, that is, the Catholic church, and the king, the absolute monarch of France. The church and the king maintained their positions by relying on the ignorance of the people. The church peddled stories of miracles and everlasting punishment in hell to keep the people in order. The kings peddled claims that they were ordained by God and that it was irreligious to question their authority; that people had no choice but to obey. One of the men of the Enlightenment summed up its program in this way: "I should like to see the last king strangled with the guts of the last priest."

Admittedly, that was an extreme view. The Enlightenment was not a revolutionary movement; it was not even a political movement. It was a collection of scholars, writers, artists, and historians who believed that as reason and education spread, superstition and ignorance would fall away and people would cease to believe in such nonsense as miracles or kings ruling by God's permission. Once you educate the people, enlightenment will follow. But the leading figures of the Enlightenment were not democrats; they were quite happy to see an enlightened ruler begin to implement their plans for a society governed by reason. Some of the monarchs of eighteenth-century Europe were, as it is said, enlightened despots. They got rid of barbaric punishments and torture; they codified their laws; they began to do something about educating the people.

The great work of the French Enlightenment was the production of an encyclopedia. It is the first great modern encyclopedia and is notable because it was not, as we think of encyclopedias today, a staid authority written by established scholars. This was a radical encyclopedia because it applied reason to everything and it gave no hierarchy within knowledge. It did not start, as the church would like, with theology and God. Where do you find God in this encyclopedia? Under D (for *Dieu*) and R (for *Religion*). This is an alphabetical index to knowledge, and that very act of making it alphabetical was a defiance of the church and its claims to possess the highest truths. All knowledge was treated in the same way and all was subjected to the same test. On adoration, the encyclopedia advised: "The manner of adoring the true God ought never to deviate from reason, because God is the author of reason . . ."

The editors had to be very careful of direct attacks on church or king because there was still a censorship operating in eighteenth-century France, though the censor was sympathetic and once suggested that the safest place to hide the plates for the next edition was in his own house! We can see how the encyclopedia navigated difficult territory by looking at the entry on Noah's Ark. It begins by asking how big Noah's Ark was. It must have been quite large. It had to accommodate not only two of each of the animals of Europe but also those of the rest of the world. And not just the animals, because being on the Ark for a long time, they needed fodder to stay alive. Two sheep would not have been enough; there would have to have been hundreds of lambs in order to feed the lions. This must have been a huge ship and yet the Bible says only four people worked to make it. How big and strong they must have been! By seeming to make a genuine inquiry the encyclopedia showed the story to be an absurdity.

The men of the Enlightenment were not necessarily opposed to God as a creator or moving spirit at the beginning of the universe. They objected to what they called superstition and how the church used it to gain control over men's minds. They hated the church's telling people that they would burn in hell if they were disobedient. The message of the Enlightenment was that *religion is superstition*. So religion, which was once central to European civilization, must be sidelined. Reason will take its place. If we follow *reason* and *science* then there will be *progress*. The arrow takes us off the page, away from darkness, toward the light.

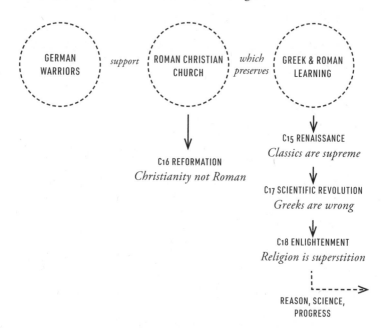

Progress was a new idea. The ancients did not believe in progress; they believed that there was a cycle of growth and decay; that institutions and society would be fresh and vigorous in their youth and then a process of corruption would set in. History would move through cycles. The church did not believe in progress, or at least not in progress by human effort independent of God, because it believed that humans were basically wicked. Humans guided solely by reason could never produce a perfect society.

THE IDEAS OF THE ENLIGHTENMENT had their first tryout in the French Revolution at the end of the eighteenth century. Sadly for the high hopes of what reason could do, the French Revolution did not bring in a new era of enlightenment when king and church were swept away; it brought bloodshed, tyranny, and dictatorship. But before that happened, the last element of the odd mixture was pulled from its moorings. This occurred with the Romantic movement of the late eighteenth and early nineteenth centuries.

The Romantic movement believed in feelings, emotions, and all the passions. In this it was directly contrary to the Enlightenment, which put its faith in reason. It was a Europe-wide movement, but strongest in Germany, where its ideas were worked out most fully. These men of the Romantic movement did not want reason to control our emotions and passions. They thought of a great writer or a great artist not as reworking in an elegant way an old theme from the classics; instead a writer or an artist should be baring his soul, bringing his passions, his anguish, and his despair to the forefront. Art should be emotional, expressive, and highly charged.

These German ideas developed in conscious opposition to the French ideas of the Enlightenment. The Germans declared that you cannot talk about man and society in the abstract because humankind is different depending on the country you are in. We are shaped, said the Romantics, by our language and our history; they are embedded in us. So the Germans, having their own history and their own language, are always going to be different from the French. There is no such thing as universal reason, which these intellectuals in French salons believe in. We are Germans and we want to find out about the Germanness of being German. The German Romantics wanted to know what the German warriors were like before they got mixed up with civilization and with Rome and Christianity. They were pulling the Germans away from the mix. They liked these men of the woods, their vigor and vitality, and their crudity. They did not want to follow weak intellectuals. They honored Germans who had lived close to the soil and who knew what being German was all about.

Our modern interest and respect for culture begins at this point, when intellectuals first began collecting folk culture. The answer to the prattle about reason by arrogant French intellectuals was to put on your boots and go hiking. Go to the German people, go to the peasants, record their stories and songs: That is where you will find true enlightenment. The message of Romanticism was that *civilization is artificial*; that it cramps and constrains us. It is within traditional culture that life is fully lived.

This view has been strong in Western society ever since. There was a great eruption of it in the 1960s. One form it takes is the cry for liberation: Let's not have any rules, let's live in a simple, direct, plain way, let's grow our own food and weave our own clothes. Let's wear our hair long, let's live in communes, let's be frank with our own feelings and frank in our dealings with each other. And let's borrow from more authentic people—from workers or peasants or "noble savages."

The Romantics also provided the ideology—the formal thinking—for nationalism, which remains a huge force in the modern world. Nationalism proclaims that distinct peoples having their own culture and language must live together and have their own government. It is not enough to work out in the abstract what makes for good government; if the government is not the government of your own people it cannot be a good government. Serbs must live together and have a Serbian government; Croats must live together and have a Croatian government. A country where Serbs and Croats live together will mean that we, as Serbs and Croats, cannot fully express ourselves. The essence of being Serb will not be able to flower unless we have our own state: This is the ideology of nationalism.

The Romantic movement believed in *emotion, culture, nationalism,* and *liberation*, an arrow moving off the chart in the opposite direction from reason, science, and progress.

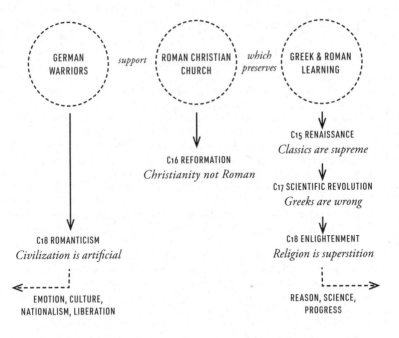

Our chart is complete. You can see what has happened in the years since 1400. There is a hole in the center where the church, which was at the center of civilization in the Middle Ages, once was. The Renaissance, the Reformation, the Scientific Revolution, the Enlightenment, and the Romantic movement: all in different ways reduced the authority of the church.

The church, that is, the Catholic church, still has some authority today, and if you are an enlightened person you might still think it worthwhile to attack the pope. Surely every enlightened person believes that birth control is a good thing, but the pope says it is against God's teaching and no pragmatic consideration can make it right. It remains wrong even if most Catholics in the West ignore the pope on this matter. But overall we have been following a great process of secularization.

The twin forces of science and progress on the one hand and emotion and liberation on the other are still very strong. Sometimes they can reinforce each other; sometimes they are opposed to each other. Consider how these two forces still divide us. First, read the account in the Bible of the creation of humankind.

> And the Lord God formed man of the dust of the ground, and breathed into his nostrils the breath of life; and man became a living soul. And the Lord God planted a garden eastward in Eden; and there he put the man whom he had formed. And the Lord God said, "It is not good that the man should be alone; I will make him a suitable helper." And the Lord God caused a deep sleep to fall upon Adam, and he slept; and he took one of his ribs, and closed up the flesh instead thereof. And the rib, which the Lord God had taken from man, made he a woman, and he brought her unto the man. And Adam said, "This is now bone of my bones, and flesh of my flesh: She shall be called Woman, because she was taken out of Man." Therefore shall a man leave his father and his mother, and shall cleave unto his wife: And they shall be one flesh.

What would you say if I were to suggest that we drop biology and evolution and teach this account in schools? "No, no," you would say, for you are an enlightened, progressive person. This is education we are talking about; if parents want their children to learn this, they can teach it to them themselves. What if we retain biology and evolution and teach the Christian account as well? "No, no." Science shows that we evolved from animals; that's all that can be taught. There are mad creationists about; we cannot afford to allow them any opening into schools.

Now read another story, an Australian Aboriginal one.

> There was once an old man who had a nephew whom he loved dearly. The young man, his nephew, went into a far country where he fell in love with a young woman. The couple ran off together, but the elders of the tribe followed them because the young woman had been promised to one of the old men of the tribe. They speared the young man and killed

him. When the old man, his uncle, heard of this he was very sad for he loved his nephew dearly. Though he was old he traveled to that country to bring the body home. The body was a great burden for the uncle, for he was truly old and the young man was almost fully grown. But he managed it; he brought the body home and it was properly buried. You can still follow the path that the old man took. Where he halted and laid the body on sandy ground, there you will find a spring. And where he laid the body on rocky ground, there you will find a rockpool, filled with the old man's tears.

Traditional Indigenous Australians live in an enchanted world. Every part of their land has its story that links their ancestors to their lives now. Do you think such stories should be preserved? "Yes," you will say. Should they be taught to Aboriginal children? "Yes, of course." Should they be taught in schools? "Yes." And they are.

Playing the role of a man of the Enlightenment, I might say, "If children want to learn about the origins of springs and rockpools, they should study geology."

"What?" you will reply. "That's not the point."

If I say, pretending still to be a man of the Enlightenment, "Indigenous Australians lived in fear of the dark and of sorcery," you are not listening. You are enchanted. The Indigenous Australians seem to have lives that are more complete, more wholesome, and more natural. You are lost to romantic feeling.

You seem to be divided. For our children you want them to have only science; yet you seem envious of those people without science, whose traditional beliefs have not been disrupted.

It is our fate to be torn, divided, and confused. Other civilizations have a single tradition and not this odd threesome. They are not so liable to the turmoil, overturnings, and confusion that we have had in our moral and intellectual life.

We come from a very mixed parentage and there is no place we can call home.

The Classic Feeling

IN THE RENAISSANCE, scholars and writers thought the art, literature, and learning of Greece and Rome might perhaps be equaled but never excelled. That is why they labeled it classic: the best. For two centuries men debated the achievements of the ancients as against the moderns. The debate was settled in the seventeenth century, when Greek science was shown to be wrong about the sun, the Earth, the planets, and the stars. From then on, there has been less reverence for the classics and more hope in what we moderns might achieve. But in some fields, our starting point remains the writers of Greece and Rome. It is still possible, as we look at these giants, to get "the classic feeling."

The three great philosophers of Athens—Socrates, Plato, and Aristotle—are still great forces in philosophy. It has been said that all Western philosophy is a footnote to Plato. The three men were intimately connected. Plato recorded the words of Socrates, who conducted philosophy as a discussion with his companions; Aristotle was Plato's pupil.

Socrates did not claim to teach the truth. He set forth the method to reach it, which was fundamentally to question everything, accept nothing at face value, and assume that ordinary opinion will have no rational basis. Socrates would ask a seemingly simple question: What is the good man? One of his companions would give a reply, which Socrates would proceed to show had a great hole in it. So this man or someone else would have another stab—but more carefully this time. There would be more questioning and more refining. Socrates believed that if your mind was clear and sharp, you could reach the truth. You didn't have to seek it out or conduct research. The truth exists; you have to cultivate your mind to grasp it.

This method still bears his name: the Socratic method. It is meant to be what happens in university tutorials, where the professor is not there to lay down the law but to help students think clearly and have a fruitful discussion. So there might be an exchange like this:

Professor: Amanda, what is a revolution?

Amanda: The overthrow of a government by force.

Professor: What if there is a state ruled by a king and the king's brother murders him and becomes king in his place—is that a revolution?

Amanda: Oh, no!

Professor: So not all cases where force is used to change governments are revolutions?

Amanda: Well, no, not all cases.

Professor: So what else is required, besides the use of force, to make a revolution?

There is a trap to this method. Clever people can do well in it without having to know very much.

Socrates, Plato, and Aristotle lived in Athens when it was a democracy, in the fifth and fourth centuries BC. They were all critics of democracy and Socrates fell foul of democratic Athens. He was put on trial for neglecting the gods and corrupting the morals of the young. His defense was that he had not insisted that anyone adopt his views; he merely questioned people so that they would have reasons for their beliefs. He was found guilty by a jury of 501 citizens, but it was a close vote. The jury then had to decide what penalty to impose. The prosecution asked for death. At this point, the accused was meant to become apologetic, to bring forward his wife and children and plead for leniency. Socrates refused to grovel. What, he asked, would be the appropriate penalty for someone who has encouraged you to improve your mental and moral well-being? Perhaps a pension for life! You might impose banishment as the penalty, but if thrown out of one town I would do the same in the next. Wherever I am, said Socrates, I cannot live without questioning: "The unexamined life is not worth living." You might impose a fine, but I have very little to offer; I am not a rich man. His followers, who had been despairing at this performance, jumped up and offered to pay a hefty fine. But the jury, not surprisingly, opted for death.

Usually executions in Athens were immediate, but this one was delayed because of a religious festival. Socrates could have escaped and the authorities probably half wished he would. But he refused this option. Why scramble, he asked, to hold on to life if I can't live forever? The aim is not to live, but to live well. I have had a good life under the laws of Athens and I am ready to accept my penalty. He remained very philosophical to the end. When his chains were taken off, he commented how close pain and pleasure are.

Execution was by the drinking of the poison hemlock. His companions pleaded with him for delay; the poison had to be drunk by the end of the day and the sun was not yet behind the hills. Socrates replied that he would make himself ridiculous in his own eyes if he clung to life. He took the poison quite calmly and with no sign of distaste. It kills very quickly.

I have told of the death of Socrates in a way that is sympathetic to the philosopher. Is it possible to tell the story so that your sympathies are with the prosecution? The prosecutor's son had attended Socrates's philosophical discussions and become a dropout and a drunk. Wasn't the prosecutor right to say Socrates was dangerous? If everything is questioned, people lose their bearings; we can't live by reason alone; there has to be custom, habit, and religion to give direction to individuals and make society possible.

This is a hard case to argue. The bias in our culture is for Socrates. It has not always been so, but Plato's account of his death has survived to make him the patron saint of questioning.

Plato is still the starting point for a central question of philosophy: Is the experience of our senses a true guide to reality? Plato believed that what we see and experience in the world are only shadowy representations of what exists in perfect form in another exalted, spiritual realm. There are ordinary tables here but there is also a table in perfect form elsewhere. Even abstract ideas like the just and the good exist in perfect form elsewhere. Humans have come from this realm; they now, by the exercise of their mind and spirit, have to rediscover it. Plato is the great idealist philosopher: He rejected a materialist account of the world.

Plato knew that common-sense people would reject his teaching; for them, he had an answer that is still powerful. Imagine a group of people shackled in front of a cave. They can't see behind them, they can only look into the cave. Behind and above them is a road and beyond the road is a large fire, which casts its light into the cave. As people, animals, and carts pass along the road, they will cast shadows on the back wall of the cave as they block out the fire's light. The shackled people will see only shadows; they will name them and discuss them; they will reason about them; they will think these shadows are the reality. Then, take one person from the cave into the open air. He will be blinded at first by the light, then confused and astounded by color and objects having three dimensions. But down there, he says, we thought . . . Yes, down there you could not see the truth.

Aristotle, Plato's pupil, was the great systematizer of knowledge about the natural world and the universe, both the Earth and the heavenly realms. In the Scientific Revolution of the seventeenth century it was his teaching, which had the Earth as the center of the universe, that was overthrown. However, Aristotle's rules about clear thinking survive. He gave us the syllogism, a three-part statement, which begins with two premises (a general and a specific statement) and then draws a conclusion. Here is an example:

> All cats have four legs
> Milligan is a cat
> *Therefore:* Milligan has four legs

Is this a correct conclusion? For a syllogism to have a correct conclusion, the two premises must be true and the argument valid. In this case, cats do indeed have four legs and Milligan, shall we say, is a cat. So the premises are true. But is the argument valid? Yes—if Milligan is a cat, and if all cats have four legs, Milligan must indeed have four legs. Here's an invalid argument about Milligan:

> All cats have four legs
> Milligan has four legs
> *Therefore:* Milligan is a cat

The conclusion is incorrect, even if the premises are true, because there is no link drawn between Milligan and cats (he could well be a dog). It is possible to have a valid argument but an incorrect conclusion; this would happen if either of the premises were not true. For example:

> All cats are black
> Milligan is a cat
> *Therefore:* Milligan is black

This argument is valid but the conclusion is incorrect because the first premise is not true. There are formal rules for identifying and naming all the ways that syllogisms can embody faulty reasoning. You can see why it is said that the Greeks taught us how to think rationally.

Modern Western medicine traces its origins to the Greeks and in particular to Hippocrates, who lived in Athens in its golden age, the fifth century BC. His writings have survived, though almost certainly they are a compilation of several authors working according to his methods and principles. Hippocrates applied reason to the understanding of disease, assuming that it had natural causes and separating it from magic, witchcraft, and divine intervention. He made a close study of the courses of diseases and the circumstances in which people caught them. In attempting to see patterns in the occurrence of disease, he was the first epidemiologist. He laid a heavy obligation on doctors to be moral, discreet people committed to the well-being of their patients; in fact, his work defined the profession of medicine. Medical students took an oath that he developed and which bore his name: the Hippocratic oath. It incidentally reveals the state of medicine in Hippocrates's day:

> The regimen I shall adopt shall be for the benefit of the patients according to my ability and judgment, and not for their hurt or for any wrong. I will give no deadly drug to any, though it be asked of me, nor will I counsel such, and especially I will not aid a woman to procure abortion. Whatsoever house I enter, there will I go for the benefit of the sick, refraining from all wrongdoing or corruption, and especially from any act of seduction, of male or female, of bond or free. Whatsoever things I see or hear concerning the life of men, in my attendance on the sick or even apart therefrom, which ought not be noised abroad, I will keep silence thereon, counting such things to be as sacred secrets. Pure and holy will I keep my life and my art.

But Hippocrates also burdened Western medicine with a great error that arose from the Greek search for simplicity. He taught that the health of the body depended on the correct balance of four elements, or humors: blood, phlegm, yellow bile, and black bile. Until the nineteenth century, this was the authority for applying leeches when too much blood was identified as the source of illness. In this regard, Hippocrates was accepted as a classic for too long.

The Greeks were superior to the Romans in nearly all branches of learning, but not in law. Roman law grew organically, with the rulings of judges and the commentaries of legal experts becoming part of what constituted the law. Though the Romans were more down-to-earth people than the Greeks, their legal thinking had more than a touch of Greek idealism. As they examined the laws of the peoples they had conquered, they were interested in finding the commonalities. What did all people agree should be the law? This line of inquiry led to the notion that there was a natural law—law in perfect form—that should be used to refine the laws of any particular society and that no society committed to justice should flout.

The most complete compendium of Roman law was assembled in the sixth century AD by the order of Emperor Justinian, who ruled the Eastern Empire, which had survived the assault of the Germans. Justinian's Code, when it was rediscovered in the eleventh century, was immensely influential. This was less so in England, whose own common law was already well established, but the English law of contract was influenced by the code. Here are two questions that relate to contract.

Consider the contract for hire. If a horse out on hire is stolen, what is the liability of the hirer? Answer: He must pay the cost of the horse to the owner because he should have taken care of it. (We now deal with this by insurance, which the Romans did not have.) But if the horse was stolen by violence, the hirer was not liable. He did not have to put himself in danger to protect someone else's horse. But if the hirer had kept the horse beyond the stipulated time, he was responsible for the loss, even if the horse was taken by violence.

Consider a goldsmith's being engaged to make a ring. Is this a contract for sale of the ring or a contract for hire of the goldsmith? Different rules applied to these different contracts. The answer depended on who supplied the gold. If the customer supplied the gold, the contract was for hire of the goldsmith. If the goldsmith supplied the gold, it was a contract for sale.

You can see how comprehensive and detailed the law was and the determination of the compilers to establish just principles in all the variety of human transactions. We might choose to do things differently, but whatever problem we face, we know that it has already been considered. Before this great intellectual edifice—the work of many minds over centuries—we feel small. That's the classic feeling.

CHAPTER 3

Invasions and Conquests

T HE GERMAN INVASION OF THE Roman Empire was the first of three great invasions. Following the Germans came the Muslims and then the Norsemen, or Vikings. After years of turmoil, European society stabilized and then itself began expanding—in crusades to the Holy Land, to drive the Muslims from Spain, and then by sea to lay claim to the world's treasures.

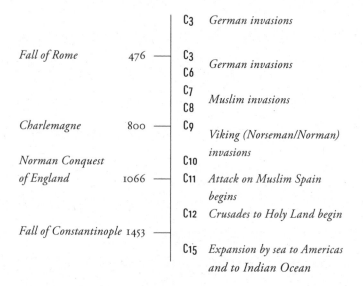

	C3	*German invasions*
Fall of Rome 476	**C3**	*German invasions*
	C6	
	C7	*Muslim invasions*
	C8	
Charlemagne 800	**C9**	
		Viking (Norseman/Norman) invasions
Norman Conquest	**C10**	
of England 1066	**C11**	*Attack on Muslim Spain begins*
	C12	*Crusades to Holy Land begin*
Fall of Constantinople 1453		
	C15	*Expansion by sea to Americas and to Indian Ocean*

We speak of the fall of the Roman Empire and we give it a date: AD 476. But only the western half of the empire fell at this time. The eastern, Greek-speaking half survived for another 1,000 years, with Constantinople as its capital. This had originally been a Greek city with the name Byzantion (in Latin, Byzantium),

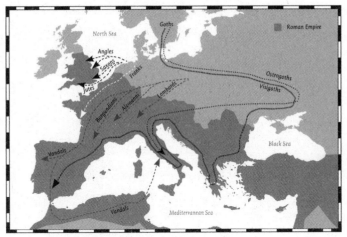

German invaders and the Roman Empire.

which gave the Eastern Empire its name: the Byzantine Empire. We will discuss its fall later.

For the western empire, "fall" gives a misleading picture—and so does a single date. There wasn't a horde of barbarians on the borders, a steady advance southward, the Romans retreating, and a last-ditch stand at Rome. It wasn't like that at all. This was a rather unusual invasion. You can follow the movements of the different German tribes on the map.

The northern borders had never been complete barriers. There had always been contact at recognized crossing places where Roman soldiers supervised the exchange of goods. Sometimes Rome had pushed beyond the usual boundaries; in the first century AD, Roman troops crossed the Rhine and advanced a long way into what is now Germany. That was a short-lived incursion because the Germans destroyed these legions, and in doing so got to know more about Rome.

In the third century AD, there had been a series of German invasions that nearly destroyed the empire. It was a time of great instability in the rule of Rome; a number of emperors came and went very quickly and very little resistance was offered to the invaders.

The empire survived but it now had enclaves of Germans settled within it. Constantine, the emperor who gave official support to Christianity in 313, followed this time of chaos and attempted generally to reorganize and strengthen the empire.

Germans settled within the empire were recruited into the Roman army so that in the battles to contain the invasions of the fifth century, Germans were fighting on both sides. Maybe half or even more of the Roman soldiers were Germans and Germans were also serving as generals. It seems a self-evident sign of the empire's weakness that Romans had to get Germans to fight for them. In the early part of the twentieth century, when racial thinking was very strong, there was a clear answer to why Rome fell: The Romans made the mistake of handing over their destiny to an inferior people. In this crude form the idea is, of course, now not entertained. But an empire relying on newcomers to defend it is not in good shape.

The Germans had no desire to take over the empire; they were invaders who did not intend to be conquerors. Their aim was to get part of the loot, to settle on land, and to live well. They were quite happy to acknowledge the rule of the emperor.

The emperors, of course, did not want them marauding through their territories. They sent forth armies to defeat or eject the invaders; only occasionally were they successful. Usually the end point was that the Germans remained in more or less independent enclaves. Finally there was very little left in the emperor's control. The Germans thought, nevertheless, that there should be an emperor. For a long time the invaders of Italy propped up a Roman as emperor. Finally one German general called an end to this farce. Instead of propping up puppets, he decided to rule openly himself. That is what happened in 476. Not a big, final battle. Odoacer, a German chieftain, took charge, but he did not call himself emperor. He called himself King of Italy. The regalia of the Emperor of the West—the crown and the great robes—he packed up and sent to Constantinople, where there was still an emperor, whose overlordship he acknowledged. The Germans were captured by the glory of what they had inadvertently conquered.

Instead of an empire in the west, there was now a series of mini-kingdoms, set up by the different German tribes. They rose and fell rapidly; they were unable to maintain the old Roman administration, so the collection of taxes soon ceased. These conquerors were basically out of their depth; they were not experienced in running any sort of settled state. They were looking for help and found it in the old Roman landed class and the bishops. The melding of old and new was happening at the top, but how far down did it go?

It is hard to know in detail because there is very little written evidence from this period. The Germans were illiterate; it was a time of turmoil and chaos and few records survive. It is clear that it was not a massive invasion, with Germans driving the existing inhabitants before them. Nor was it a raid of male warriors. The Germans brought their women and children with them and intended to settle. In some places they formed dense settlements; in others they were scattered quite thinly. To establish who settled where, historians have called on archaeological evidence. The Germans buried people in a different way from the Romans, so if many of the dead are buried in the German way, then German settlement can be assumed to have been fairly dense. Linguists can also help. If a name of a village changes at this time to something German, the assumption is that this was a dense German settlement. But perhaps this evidence is not strong enough; it might have taken only one German warlord to say the name was going to change. But if the names of the fields change, this is better evidence. It is actually the Germans who were doing the work in this part of the world.

For a time, Roman law and German law operated alongside each other. You were tried according to your ethnic origin. Roman law had clear principles of justice, which judges applied in particular cases. The early judges were makers of the law and their decisions were then gathered into codes; the greatest was assembled by the eastern emperor, Justinian, in the sixth century. German law, on the other hand, was a regularized form of vendetta, with judges monitoring the dispute. Injured parties and their kin sought recompense from offenders and their kin. Even in cases of murder, the matter was settled by payment to the kin of the murdered person—how great the payment depending on the status of the victim, an aristocrat being worth three times an ordinary person.

The Romans established guilt or innocence by the examination of evidence and witnesses, the Germans in trial by ordeal of fire, water, or battle. For example, a suspect's arm was placed in boiling water; if the arm was not healed after three days, the suspect was guilty. Suspects were thrown into water; if they floated they were guilty, and if they sank they were innocent. Two parties in dispute over land would engage in battle, and the winner declared to be in the right.

Gradually the two systems merged into one. Roman law held greater sway in the mix in Italy and southern France, German law in northern France. Everywhere, the trial by ordeal operated with priests present to ensure that God produced the correct outcome. In this matter the Roman church went the German way until the twelfth century, when the church was influenced by the rediscovery of Emperor Justinian's Code and priests were told not to participate in ordeals.

The Germans became Christian soon after the invasion, giving up their own gods and in other cases giving up Arianism, a heretical version of Christianity to which some Germans had been converted before the invasions. Arians believed that since Jesus was the son of God, he must be a lesser person and could not be the equal of God. For a time this heresy was strong in the east and was carried to the Germans by the missionary who had converted them.

So in many ways the "fall of Rome" is misleading, and most misleading in regard to religion: The official religion of the Roman Empire and its church survived, and both were embraced by the invaders. This is the foundation point of European civilization. We already have a formulation to embody it: German warriors supported a Roman Christian church, which preserved Greek and Roman learning.

ONLY ONE GERMAN TRIBE IN THE WEST produced a long-lasting state; this was the kingdom of the Franks, which grew, as you see on the map, to cover modern France and parts of Germany, Spain, and Italy. The name "France" derives from the Franks and hence is German in origin. The Frankish kingdom reached its greatest extent under the rule of Charles the Great, or Charlemagne. After his death, the kingdom broke up. Modern France is not the direct descendant of the Frankish kingdom; France as we know it had to be put slowly together by its later kings.

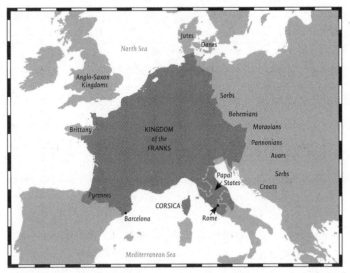

The kingdom of the Franks grew to cover modern France and parts of Germany, Spain, and Italy.

The German invasion of Britain took a different form. Most of modern England was in the Roman Empire; Scotland was not. The Romans went to Britain late—only in the first century AD—and they departed early. They left in AD 410 because the emperor wanted the troops stationed there brought back to defend the empire against the Germans. When the Romans left, the native society of the Britons was still intact; it had not been obliterated by 300 years of Roman settlement. The Celtic language survived. Then in the fifth and sixth centuries, German peoples—the Angles, Saxons, and Jutes—crossed the Channel and invaded England. This was more like a complete conquest. The Britons were overrun and their societies survived only in Scotland, Wales, and Cornwall.

England became a completely German society, with a number of separate kingdoms, and pagan. The Angles, Saxons, and Jutes were not Christians of any sort. Then, from Ireland and from Rome, missionaries went to England to convert these newcomers to Christianity. The role of Ireland in the conversion of England is one of the amazing stories of the survival of Christianity. Christianity began in the far east of the Roman Empire; from there it spread throughout the empire; it then jumped the empire's boundaries and reached Ireland. Here, it became Christianity of a special sort because it operated in a society that was not Roman. When the empire in the west was invaded, the Irish were safe; they then re-Christianized England and sent missionaries to Europe as well. The English came to look down on the Irish as "Bog Irish"; the Irish know themselves to be the saviors of Christendom.

The next great invasion was Islamic. It occurred in the seventh and eighth centuries, the two centuries immediately after the German invasions. The founder of the Islamic religion was Muhammad, a merchant in Arabia who received visions from God. The religion he developed by divine prompting is an offshoot of Judaism and Christianity. Islam accepts Jesus and the Jewish prophets before him as true prophets but claims Muhammad is the last of the prophets, the true guide to Allah, the one God. Islam is a much simpler religion than Christianity; it lacks the Greek cleverness that gave Christianity a three-person god—Father, Son, and Holy Ghost—separate but equal, separate but one. In Islam, God is the single Allah. Muslims were quite tolerant of Christians and Jews. Christians, on the other hand, regarded Muslims as deceivers and destroyers of the true faith.

Muhammad won over Arabia for his new faith by conquering its pagan tribes and forcing them to submit. In his life he was a more influential figure than Jesus: he founded a religion and established it in a wide territory. At the time of Jesus's death, there was nothing of Christianity. After Muhammad's death, his followers

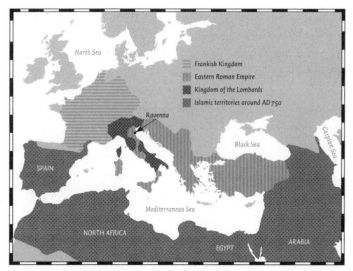

The Muslim advance. Of the Eastern Roman Empire only the Balkans and modern-day Turkey survived. The Eastern Empire had also acquired territory in Italy, which had of course been part of the western empire. Italy had been invaded by Germans, but then the emperor in Constantinople thought it his Christian duty to recapture these lands. He regained small enclaves but at great cost. There was far more chaos and bloodshed caused by the attempt at reconquest than by the German invasions. Ravenna in northern Italy was one of the enclaves, which explains why that city still possesses beautiful Byzantine mosaics.

continued the conquests with even greater success. In short order they conquered not only tribes but established states, the Persian Empire, and then a good deal of the Eastern Roman Empire in the Middle East and North Africa. They continued westward along North Africa, now conquering states that had been established by German invaders, and then crossed into Spain. This had been a Roman province, then was invaded by the Visigoths, who became Christian, and now it was Islamic. Here the conquests stopped. A Muslim army advanced well into France but was defeated at Tours by Charles Martel, leader of the Franks and grandfather of Charlemagne. The Franks saved Europe for Christianity.

The Muslims were ruthless conquerors of Christians, but gentle rulers. They allowed Christians to continue their worship, but as non-believers they had to pay a tax; Muslims paid no tax. This was an incentive to convert to Islam. The Christians in the Eastern Roman Empire half welcomed the Muslims because they were upset at the version of Christianity that Constantinople was insisting they follow. Under the Muslims they could practice what they liked, but gradually Christianity died out in these lands. As more and more people converted to Islam, of course, the rule about tax had to be changed; everyone soon paid a tax on land in the normal way.

Spain under Muslim rule became, in the Middle Ages, the most civilized part of Europe. On their journeys of conquest, the illiterate Arab tribesmen had learned from the people they conquered: from the Persians, who sustained a highly cultivated civilization, and from the Greeks in the Byzantine Empire. The Arabs carried the Greek learning with them to Spain, recorded and elaborated on it, and allowed scholars from Northern Europe to come and make copies. The Jews, who held high positions in Muslim Spain, were often the translators. One person reading the document in Arabic (into which it had been previously translated from the Greek) translated it aloud into Spanish. A second person hearing the Spanish made a written draft in Latin. In its new Latin version,

Greek learning, having been through three translations, was taken back to be studied in the universities of Christian Europe, which began to operate from the twelfth century. In this way, Western Europe acquired Aristotle's writings on logic and works on medicine, astronomy, and math—the disciplines in which the Greeks were masters.

Let us summarize the outcome of three conquests. First, in Western Europe a melding of German and old Roman and Christian. Second, in England a complete German takeover and then a reconversion to Christianity. Third, in the Muslim world—in the Middle East, North Africa, and Spain—Christianity died out but Greek learning was preserved and transmitted to Christian Europe.

THE VIKINGS OR NORSEMEN were the last of the invaders, marauding through Europe in the ninth and tenth centuries, the two centuries immediately following the Muslim advance. Their homes were in the north—Sweden, Norway, and Denmark—and they came by sea. Their great longboats were a terrifying sight. They

A Viking longboat. Its shallow draft enabled inland raids up rivers.

had a very shallow draft—they needed only about three feet of water under them—so they could sail a long way up the rivers. If the river got very shallow, they would launch small boats, which they carried with them, and continue. If they met some sort of barrier, they carried their boat around it and kept rowing. They penetrated far inland; in Russia they traveled from the Baltic to the Black Sea.

Their open boats could sail on the ocean only in summer. At first they came for the summer and then returned home. Their aim was plunder: precious objects, things they could carry back with them. But while they were looking for precious objects, they plundered to survive, seizing food, horses, women, and taking more than they needed. They were determined terrorists. Not just raiding and robbing but plundering on a large scale, burning and looting; even things they could not carry away with them they destroyed. Their aim was to create total panic. People fled before them and they were merciless. In one of their sagas there was a warrior referred to as the children's man because he refused to impale children on the point of his lance.

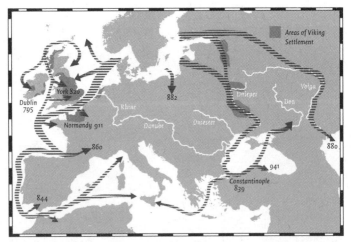

The Vikings, or Norsemen, marauded through Europe in the ninth and tenth centuries.

The Germans had come by land. The safest place from marauders seemed to be islands in rivers or offshore. Monasteries had been built in these places and now they were easily plundered by these sea-going raiders. Monasteries were highly attractive because they held precious objects made of gold and silver and great quantities of food, for they were a sort of agribusiness, growing and storing enough food for one or two hundred monks. At the mouth of the River Loire in France was a monastery on an offshore island. Every summer the monks would move further inland up the river, but the Vikings chased them in their longboats. The monastery moved about four or five times up the Loire and finally came to rest in what is now Switzerland, with the monks carrying their crosses of gold and their piece of the True Cross and portion of Christ's leg.

The Norsemen could range so widely without opposition because governments were weak; they had no regular system of tax, and while they could put an army together, these invaders did not come by land. None of these little Western European kingdoms had a navy. Charlemagne never had a navy, and his empire, in any case, was gone. The Roman Empire had used the sea— the Mediterranean Sea held it together—but now a large part of that sea was in Muslim hands. In the states of Europe there was little trade carried by sea and the art of sailing was lost; Europe was turned inward—and hence was vulnerable to a highly mobile invading force.

After a time the Norsemen brought their wives and children and settled permanently. The map shows their settlements, in Russia, northern France, England, and Ireland. Dublin was originally a Norse city. England had a double dose of invasions: first the Angles, Saxons, and Jutes, and then the Norsemen on the eastern side of the island. Both groups of invaders spoke Germanic languages, from which English derives. The settlement in northern France took its name, Normandy, from its Norse inhabitants. The French king let them settle there on the condition that they stopped their raiding.

About 100 years after the Normans had settled in northern France, the Norman duke William with a few of his followers conquered England in the year 1066. This was just a takeover from the top; Duke William and his followers installed themselves as the new ruling class in England. The Normans spoke their own form of French, which then became part of the mix that formed English. England was a society of invaders, but after 1066 the country has not been invaded again.

After the tenth century, the incursions into Europe stopped. The Normans were persuaded to settle, and missionaries went to Norway and Sweden and converted those countries to Christianity. Trade revived and towns expanded. European society was now stable and strong enough to send out its own expeditions.

The first task Christendom undertook was to drive back the Muslims. These were Europe-wide campaigns directed first to the reconquest of Spain and then to recapturing the Holy Land of Palestine. The reconquest of Spain began in the eleventh century and took over 400 years to complete. It proceeded in installments; coming from the north, the Christians seized a wide swath of territory, reestablished a Christian society, and then pushed south again. The last Muslims were driven from southern Spain in 1492, the same year that Columbus, under the patronage of Spanish monarchs, sailed westward.

The crusades to the Holy Land began in 1095 and went on for almost two centuries. Imagine what it meant to Christians to know that the place where Christ died, the country where he taught, was in the hands of people whom they regarded as infidels and the active enemies of their religion. God must want them to remove this blasphemy. The pope encouraged and sanctioned the crusades. But only the first of these had any measure of success. Jerusalem was briefly regained for Christ and some of the crusaders made permanent settlements. Then the Muslims drove them out and all the subsequent crusades failed.

Crusades were cooperative efforts. By contrast, the expansion overseas to America and Asia from the fifteenth century was a competition among emerging nation-states: first Spain and Portugal, then Britain, France, and Holland. The first aim was to reach the spices and other riches of Asia. There were two routes: by sea around southern Africa, or westward across the Atlantic. When he came across America, Columbus was intending to reach China. It was more than ample compensation for this disappointment that the Spanish monarchy, which had sponsored him, gained access to the gold and silver of Central and South America. The Portuguese were the first to arrive in Asia; they were pushed aside by the French and English, who contested for the control of India, and by the Dutch, who wrested control of the East Indies (now Indonesia).

Luxury goods from Asia had long been reaching Europe, but they came from the east through the great capital of the Byzantine Empire, Constantinople. Europeans took to the oceans partly because the route to the east had fallen into Muslim hands.

This was more truly a "fall." The Eastern Roman Empire had survived in the fifth century because the Germans had concentrated their attack on the west. The Eastern Empire may have also had a stronger economy and administration. However, it steadily began losing territory. A great slice went to the Muslim invaders coming out of Arabia in the seventh and eighth centuries. Then, in the ninth century, the Turks rode out of the Asian steppes; they converted to Islam on their way south and west, and established their rule through the Middle East, seizing what is modern Turkey from the Byzantines. They crossed into Europe and finally held territory on all sides of Constantinople. They captured the city itself in 1453. The last Byzantine emperor died fighting alongside his troops.

And so the Roman Empire, reduced to a patch of territory and more Greek than Roman, came to an end. The great cathedral of Hagia Sophia (Holy Wisdom), built by Emperor Justinian in the

Hagia Sophia, a cathedral built by Emperor Justinian in the sixth
century AD, was converted to a mosque and is now a museum.

sixth century, was converted into a mosque. The Turks themselves
ran an empire, the Ottoman Empire. When it came to an end
after World War I, modern Turkey was established as a secular
state, though most of its people are Muslim. The great mosque
that had been built as a church was turned into a museum.

With the fall of Constantinople, Christian scholars who
had preserved and studied the learning of classical Greece took
themselves and their manuscripts to Italy. They were very readily
received because in the Renaissance scholars were hunting for
ancient manuscripts. Even before 1453, scholars in Italy had made
contact with scholars in Constantinople to gain access to Greek
learning and literature. Latin learning and literature had been
preserved continuously in western Europe. Some Greek learning
was preserved in Latin, and although the whole of Roman literature had been influenced by the Greeks, the Greek originals
only arrived after a long interval and from the extremities—from
Spain in the Middle Ages and from Constantinople in the fifteenth century.

CHAPTER 4

Forms of Government I

THE ANCIENT GREEKS INVENTED THE democratic state. They also invented politics, a word that comes from their word for city, *polis*. There had long been governments of various sorts; the Greeks invented government by discussion among all citizens and majority voting. Theirs was direct democracy in which all citizens gathered in one place to debate and determine policy. Not all the Greek city-states were democracies, and democracies were always precarious. Of all the little democratic states, we know most about Athens, where democracy survived, with some interruptions, for 170 years. During this time, all the men born in Athens had the right to participate in government, but not women or slaves.

We call our system democracy but it is very different from Athenian democracy; ours is representative democracy. We are not regularly involved in the process of government. We vote every couple of years; we have the opportunity to complain and stage demonstrations and make submissions, but we do not directly vote on every issue that comes before our representatives.

If the people were directly in charge of our democracy, we know it would be a very different system from what we have. Of course, not all the people could gather in one place but we could reproduce the Greek system if, on every issue, there was a referendum conducted on the internet. With such a system—simple majority rule—we know that there's a real risk of endangering the rights of minorities and the disadvantaged, with a potentially wide range of consequences. Xenophobic immigration policies might permanently reign; cruel and unusual punishment of criminals might persist; overseas aid might not exist; single parents might struggle to keep any form of government assistance; students would probably struggle to keep their benefits. So you might think it is fair that the ignorance and the prejudice of the people do not have free rein.

If you have come to that position you are now close to the view of Socrates, Plato, and Aristotle, the great Athenian philosophers, who had severe doubts about Athenian democracy and whose criticisms help us to understand how it operated. They complained that the people were fickle; they were indecisive; they were ignorant; they were easily swayed. Government is a fine art that requires wisdom and judgment, which are not the possession of all citizens. The philosophers would be much happier with our system of representative democracy. No matter what we say about our representatives, they are usually better educated and better informed than the people as a whole. Our politicians are guided by a civil service in which there are very able people. So the people do not rule directly and there is an input from those who are trained and reflective about the whole business of government. But Socrates, Plato, and Aristotle would not call our system democracy.

The origins of Greek democracy lay in the army. As we examine the different forms of government we will notice a connection between the nature of military power and the nature of the state. In Athens there was no regular full-time army, no "standing army" as the term is—an army in barracks that can be called on to fight at any time. In Athens, all the soldiers were part-time, but rigorously trained to fight on foot in close formation. When war was declared, citizens left their normal business as tradespeople or farmers and constituted the army. The democratic assembly began its life as citizen-soldiers gathered together to get their marching orders from their leaders. The decisions about war or peace and tactics had already been made by the council of elders, the nobility of the tribe. They were then laid before the mass of the soldiers. The aim was to put them in the picture, to psych them up. The assembly of soldiers was not to debate the matter or to propose anything different; they were meant to shout their approval and sing their battle songs.

Gradually, the assembly gained more power and eventually complete control. We don't know fully how this came about, but since the state relied on the participation of its citizen-soldiers, and since wars were very regular events, the soldiers were in a strong position. So the democracy began as a solidarity of fighting men. But it was also tribal. There were initially four tribes in Athens and they used to come together to fight as separate tribes. Tribes elected the offices of government, and even when Athens became a more formal democracy and drew up electorates, you remained in your electorate for life, even if you moved to live somewhere else. So geography alone never seemed a strong enough bond; you had a lifelong tie with those you voted with.

DIRECT DEMOCRACY REQUIRED a great commitment from the people and a great faith in the people. The ideals of Athenian democracy were set forth by Pericles, the leader of Athens, in a speech he gave at the burial of soldiers killed in a war against Sparta. This "funeral oration" is recorded in *The Peloponnesian War* by the Athenian author Thucydides, the first historian who attempted to be objective and fair-minded. Thucydides's history was preserved in manuscript at Constantinople. In the Renaissance, 1,800 years after it was written, it reached Italy and was translated into Latin and then into modern European languages. After Lincoln's Gettysburg Address, it is the most famous speech of a politician at a cemetery. Pericles's speech was much longer than Lincoln's. These are only extracts:

> Our constitution is called a democracy because power is in the hands not of a minority but of the whole people. When it is a question of settling private disputes, everyone is equal before the law; when it is a question of putting one person before another in positions of public responsibility, what counts is not membership of a particular class, but the actual ability that the man possesses.

When our work is over, we are in a position to enjoy all kinds of recreation for our spirits. There are various kinds of contests and sacrifices regularly throughout the year; in our own homes we find a beauty and good taste that delight us every day and that drive away cares.

Here each individual is interested not only in his own affairs but in the affairs of the state as well; even those who are mostly occupied with their own business are extremely well informed on general politics—this is a peculiarity of ours: We do not say that a man who takes no interest in politics is a man who minds his own business; we say that he has no business here at all.

An open, cultivated society with committed, engaged citizens: This is an attractive ideal now to anyone who cares about democracy, even though we know that Athenian leisure and beauty rested on slavery and that sometimes citizens had to be herded into the assembly. However, the positive influence of Pericles's speech was long delayed. For centuries, the elite of Europe had not only their interests but also their education to warn them against democracy, since most of the classical authors they read were hostile to it. So much so that in the early nineteenth century an English scholar and radical, George Grote, produced a new study of Greece to argue that the democracy and the high culture were interconnected and you could not damn the one and accept the other. This was his contribution to the cause of democracy in England.

Even to us there are some aspects of Greek democracy that are at odds with our ideals. It was very communal and a touch coercive; there was little sense of individual rights. The privilege of an Athenian citizen was to belong—as Pericles said, if you are not interested in politics you have no business here. Our concern with individual rights has other origins.

Athens and all the other little Greek states lost their independence when Alexander the Great, the ruler of Macedonia in northern Greece, took them over early in the fourth century BC. Democracy was lost, but not the Greek culture that had flourished in Athens. It spread with Alexander's empire, which extended throughout the eastern Mediterranean and into the Middle East. What Alexander had made into a Greek world remained so when it was conquered by Rome and became the eastern, Greek-speaking half of its empire.

When Rome began its expansion, it was a republic but not a democracy. There were popular assemblies that began, like those in the Greek states, as a group of armed men. Every citizen in Rome had to fight and supply their own equipment and weapons. You contributed according to your wealth. If you were rich, you supplied a horse and joined the cavalry, which was a fairly small section of the Roman army. All the rest were foot soldiers but of different grades: The first came fully armed with a sword, a coat of mail, and a shield; the next had less armor; the third had only a spear or a javelin; and the last class of infantry—the poorest people—could afford only a sling, a bit of cloth or leather with which you could hurl a stone.

In the early years, the assembly was like an army on a parade ground. Men were drawn up in their different ranks: cavalry, first-class foot soldiers, second, third, fourth, down to the people with slings. The voting took place by groups. So all the cavalry decided their view of the matter by internal discussion; all the first-class infantry decided their view of the matter, and so on. Each group expressed a joint opinion, but their voting power was not equal. There were 193 votes overall, and these were allocated to the groups according to their status. The cavalry and the first-class infantry-men together had 98 votes out of a possible 193 votes, which is a majority, though the bulk of the soldiers were in the lesser groups. If these first two groups agreed, there was no need even to ask the others, and often they were not asked; the horsemen and the first-class soldiers had settled the matter. All men potentially at least participated, but the rich had the predominant voice.

This assembly elected the Roman consuls, who were the co-presidents of the republic; there were two of them and they could act only if they agreed. The two consuls controlled each other, and their power was further limited by holding office for only one year. Romans identified the years by the persons who had been consuls.

Gradually, the common people claimed more power for themselves in comparison to the wealthy and the nobles. We do know how this happened—they used their military power to get it. A war would be declared and the common soldiers, ranks three, four, and five, refused to fight. They said we will fight only if you give us more power in the state. They used that threat to obtain a new assembly, one that appointed officers called tribunes, who had power to intervene at any stage in the governmental process if an ordinary person was getting a raw deal. After another refusal to fight, this assembly was given a strong role in law-making.

Sometimes these actions are referred to as strikes, which is a poor word for them. Strikes suggest that this process was taking place in the sphere of industrial relations, that working people were being unionized in Rome and were calling strikes against their bosses. It was not like that at all. The common people staged a mutiny. Their opportunity came not out of industrial relations but international relations.

As in Athens, citizen-soldiers increased their power, except that in Rome, democracy never fully triumphed. The chief body in Rome remained the Senate, which was composed of members from noble families and later more from wealthy families. The popular assemblies with their increased power put limits on the Senate but did not overawe or supplant it. The Roman constitution changed by the creation of new institutions and shifts in the relations of power, not by revolution and a fresh start. In this, it was followed by the British constitution, which has still not been written down in one document. In its concern to have power dispersed and checked, the Roman constitution was an important model for that of the United States.

THE ROMANS HAD FIRST BEEN RULED by kings. The republic was only established in about 500 BC when the Romans overthrew the tyrant king, Tarquin the Proud. The Roman historian Livy gives an account of this revolt. His work was preserved in Western Europe after the fall of Rome but some of it had disappeared; only a single copy of one section survived and was not discovered until the sixteenth century, so it remained unknown to Renaissance scholars. The section dealing with the establishment of the republic was known. Shakespeare drew on it for his poem "The Rape of Lucrece."

It was a rape that sparked the republican revolt. The rapist was not Tarquin himself but his son, Sextus Tarquinius. His victim was Lucretia, the wife of Collatinus. The leader of the revolt that expelled the king was Brutus, who was a nephew of the king. His namesake 400 years later led the plot to assassinate Julius Caesar. The first Brutus had seen many of his family killed by Tarquin the Proud. To survive, Brutus had pretended to be a sort of half-wit, otherwise Tarquin would have done away with him as well. Brutus was being true to his name, which in Latin means "dull-witted." He made no complaint when Tarquin seized all his property. He was biding his time, and his opportunity came with the rape of Lucretia. This is the story as Livy tells it. It begins when the sons of the king are away from Rome at Ardea fighting a war. Collatinus was drinking with them in their tent when they started to talk about their wives, with each boasting that his wife was the best. Collatinus suggested that they settle the matter by riding back to Rome to check on what their wives were doing. The wives of the princes were found partying, but Lucretia was hard at work, spinning. Collatinus had won the argument. A few days later, Sextus, without Collatinus's knowledge, returned to visit Lucretia.

He was hospitably welcomed in Lucretia's house and, after supper, escorted, like the honored visitor he was thought to be, to the guest chamber. Here he waited till the house was asleep and then, when all was quiet, he drew his sword and made his way to Lucretia's room determined to rape her. She was asleep. Laying his left hand on her breast, "Lucretia," he whispered, "not a sound. I am Sextus Tarquinius, I am armed—if you utter a word I will kill you." Lucretia opened her eyes in terror; death was imminent, no help at hand. Sextus urged his love, begged her to submit, pleaded, threatened, used every weapon that might conquer a woman's heart. But all in vain; not even the fear of death could bend her will. "If death will not move you," Sextus cried, "dishonor shall. I will kill you first, then cut the throat of a slave and lay his naked body by your side. Then everyone will believe that you have been caught in adultery with a servant and paid the price." Even the most resolute chastity could not have stood against this dreadful threat.

Lucretia yielded. Sextus enjoyed her and rode away, proud of his success.

The unhappy girl wrote to her father in Rome and to her husband in Ardea, urging them both to come at once with a trusted friend and quickly, for a frightful thing had happened. Her father came with Valerius, her husband with Brutus, with whom he was returning to Rome when he was met by the messenger. They found Lucretia sitting in her room in deep distress. Tears rose to her eyes as they entered and to her husband's question, "Is it well with you?" she answered, "No, what can be well with a woman who has lost her honor? In your bed, Collatinus, is the impress of another man. My body only has been violated; my heart is innocent and death will be my witness. Give me your solemn promise that the adulterer shall be punished. He is Sextus Tarquinius. He it is who last night came as my enemy disguised as my guest and took his pleasure of me. That pleasure will be my death—and his too if you are men."

The promise was given. One after another they tried to comfort her, they told her she was helpless and therefore innocent, that he alone was guilty. It was the mind, they said, that sinned, not the body: Without intention there could never be guilt.

"What is due to him," Lucretia said, "is for you to decide. As for me, I am innocent of fault but I will take my punishment. Never shall Lucretia provide a precedent for unchaste women to escape what they deserve." With these words she drew a knife from under her robe, drove it into her heart, and fell forward, dead. Her father and her husband were overwhelmed with grief. While they stood weeping helplessly, Brutus drew the bloody knife from Lucretia's body and, holding it before him, cried: "By this girl's blood—none more chaste till a tyrant wronged her—and by the gods I swear that with sword and fire and whatever else can lend strength to my arm, I will pursue Lucius Tarquinius the Proud, his wicked wife, and all his children, and never again will I let them or any other man be king in Rome."

Brutus was true to his word. So the republic was launched because of an outrageous crime by a prince; because a woman, like a good Roman, valued her honor more highly than her life; and because one man was determined to avenge her. But not everyone in Rome wanted Tarquin off the throne, and there was a conspiracy to bring the king back. When the conspiracy was uncovered, Brutus was one of the first two consuls, the officeholders who had replaced the king. Brutus was sitting in the public assembly, in the seat of judgment, when the names of the conspirators were brought before him. On the list were two of his sons. It was Brutus's job to pass sentence of punishment on them. People in the crowd yelled out that they did not want his family to be so dishonored; that he could pardon his sons. But Brutus would not hear of it; the same rule was going to apply to his sons as to everyone else. So while Brutus watched, his sons were stripped naked, flogged, and then beheaded. He did not flinch. Such was his devotion to the republic.

Jacques-Louis David, *The Lictors Bring to Brutus the Bodies of His Sons*, 1789.

The Romans of course praised Brutus; this is the very essence of devotion to the republic: that you will put all personal and private ties aside and serve the public good. This is what the Romans called *virtus*, republican virtue, necessary if the republic was to survive without the tie of allegiance to a king. You might think that Brutus was inhuman; how could he sit there and have that done to his own children? This republican virtue created monsters.

Strangely, just before the revolution in France, there was a cult of admiration for republican Rome—and not just among those who wanted to reform the monarchy. The court painter to Louis XVI, Jacques-Louis David, took as his subjects two famous episodes from Livy. In the first, he depicted Brutus not in the judgment seat condemning his sons, but at home when the decapitated bodies were brought in. This allowed David to contrast the unmoved, implacable father staring straight ahead with the weakness of women, the mother and sisters of the deceased, who are weeping over their loss. David's second tribute to republican virtue was the painting called *The Oath of the Horatii*.

The Horatii were the three sons of Horatius who were chosen to fight as champions of Rome when Rome and one of its enemies resolved not to fight in battle but to allow their dispute to be settled by three men from each side fighting each other. David, in his painting, shows the father swearing his sons to their allegiance to Rome. They are placing their hands on their swords and raising their arms in the republican salute, which took the same form as the Nazi salute. The women—the mother and the sisters of the soldiers—again display their human weakness by weeping as the young men depart. One sister is particularly distressed because she is engaged to one of the champions who is going to fight for the other side.

It was a ferocious, terrifying battle, a battle to the death, wonderfully described by Livy. Only one man survives, one of the sons of Horatius, so Rome has won. The victor comes home and finds his sister crying because her fiancé is dead, killed by her brother. The brother takes out his sword and runs it through his sister; kills her, for weeping when she should have been rejoicing at his own and Rome's success. Again the message is that family has to be sacrificed in the service of the state. The brother is put on trial but is quickly found to be not guilty. The father turns up at the trial, criticizes his daughter, and so helps to free his son.

Jacques-Louis David, *The Oath of the Horatii*, 1784.

THE ROMAN REPUBLIC LASTED for a couple of hundred years and then it began to fall into disorder. Rome had expanded; its great generals, who had made its conquests, became rivals and began to fight each other. Their soldiers were loyal to them rather than to the republic. One great general emerged and conquered all the others: Julius Caesar. The second Brutus organized the assassination of Caesar to save the republic from one-man rule, but that deed simply led to another round of civil wars between Brutus and his fellow conspirators on one side and the friends of Caesar on the other. One man emerged victorious: Caesar's grandnephew and adopted son, who in 27 BC made himself into Rome's first emperor under the name Augustus.

Augustus was very astute. He kept the republican institutions; the assemblies still met and consuls were still elected. He called himself not "emperor" but "first citizen." He saw his job as a sort of facilitator, or he pretended he was a facilitator, just helping the machinery work properly. There was no great pomp; he did not have a great escort; he walked around Rome like an ordinary citizen without a bodyguard; he went into the Senate, which was still meeting, and listened to the debates; he was personally very accessible. The form of greeting and the way you showed your allegiance remained the raised-arm salute. When you came into Augustus's presence. you did not have to bow or show any deference; you and the emperor saluted each other.

Augustus tried to revive the old Roman virtues. He thought Rome had been undermined by luxury and

Augustus became Rome's first emperor in 27 BC.

THE SHORTEST HISTORY OF EUROPE

decadence; he wanted to restore, as we would say, family values. He banished the poet Ovid for writing that women who had children were no longer so beautiful. He was critical of Livy, the historian, who was writing at this time, because he did not like some of what Livy had written about the disputes in Rome's recent past, but he was with Livy on the Roman virtues: noble conduct and devotion to the state. But one Roman practice he could not revive. Rome now had an empire that Augustus stabilized and ruled well but with the help, not of part-time citizen-soldiers, but of a paid standing army.

For two centuries the empire enjoyed peace. Over its vast area, Roman law and Roman order prevailed. In form, the empire was still a republic: Emperors did not become like kings, whose heirs would be kings after them. The emperor chose a successor, who might or might not be a relative, and the Senate would approve the choice. Later there would be bloody conflicts between rival claimants, but for two centuries emperors mostly chose well and their choice was accepted.

Then in the third century AD came the first wave of German invasions, which nearly brought the empire down. After the invasions had passed, the empire was reconstructed on new lines by two emperors, Diocletian and Constantine. To shore up the empire's defenses, they enlarged and reorganized the army, recruiting many of the Germans who had settled within the borders. To pay for a larger army, the emperors had to raise taxes. To ensure that people paid their taxes, they had to have a more accurate registration of the population. So the bureaucracy grew and the bureaucrats became the direct rulers of the empire. In earlier times, the different regions were allowed to run themselves so long as peace was kept and taxes paid.

Diocletian attempted to control inflation by making death the punishment for raising prices. Taxes went up to pay for a larger army, but if you were in business you were not allowed to raise your prices to help pay for the taxes. So you might think it is not worth being in business anymore. Diocletian had an answer for that: You were obliged to stay in your business and your son had to carry on the business after you. The emperors were now desperate; they were not ruling a society but coercing it. A society governed in this way did not have the resilience or morale to resist the next wave of invasions.

Constantine's official support for Christianity in 313 was part of the attempt to strengthen the empire. The strength he sought did not lie in the church as an organization; Christianity had grown but it was still a minority faith. Constantine, like many of his subjects, was losing faith in the old Roman gods, and he came to believe that the Christian god would best protect him and the empire. At first, he had only the vaguest idea of what being a Christian entailed, but he thought that if he supported the Christians then their god would favor him.

Diocletian, Constantine, and the later emperors became increasingly remote. They began to imitate the Persian emperors and to present themselves as godlike figures. They stayed in their palaces; they were never seen walking around their cities as Augustus had. Before you went in to visit them, you were frisked. You were taken blindfolded through a great labyrinth of passages so you would never know your way in again, in case you had it in mind to assassinate the emperor. When finally you got to see the emperor, you had to prostrate yourself; that is, you lay flat on the floor before the throne.

As Rome exerted tighter control, its subjects sought ways to escape. The great landowners, not wanting to pay tax themselves, became islands of resistance, protecting also the people who worked their lands. In the early years of the empire, these were slaves. When the supply of slaves dried up—because Rome's conquests had ceased—the landowners divided up their lands and rented them out to slaves, ex-slaves, and free men who sought their protection. Though the landowners resented (and avoided) paying taxes to the later emperors, they embraced the emperors' new laws that people

	Military Organization	Political Context	Form of Greeting
CLASSICAL	Citizen-soldiers	500 BC Greek democracy Roman Republic	Republican salute
	Paid foot soldiers	27 BC Augustus, first Roman Emperor	Republican salute
	Paid foreign foot soldiers	Diocletian, Constantine, Late empire 476 Fall of Rome	Prone

had to stay where they were and that any tenant seeking to move could be chained up. The tenants of different origins were coming to assume the same status—they were becoming what were known in the Middle Ages as serfs. They were not owned like slaves, and they had their own plot of ground and a family, but they could not leave and were bound to work for and support their lord.

Medieval society was taking shape before AD 476, the date we give for the fall of the empire in the west. There were already great landowners living in fortified houses, the masters and protectors of the people who worked their lands. The societies that replaced the empire in the west were to be held together by personal allegiance, not allegiance to the state, whether republic or empire. But Roman rule had a continuous afterlife in the memory of Europe.

CHAPTER 5

Forms of Government II

T HE STATES THAT REPLACED the Roman Empire in the west were very primitive. The basis of the state was that the king, formerly a warrior chief, gave out land to his followers, and in return the followers were obliged to provide him with a fighting force. So the king gained his army without taxation or any elaborate machinery of government. Land held in this way came to be called a fief, and from that word we get the word *feudum* in Latin, from which we get the English word "feudal."

Feudal monarchs, relying so heavily on what their great landowning subjects could provide, were necessarily weak monarchs. Theoretically, they kept control of the land they had allocated, but in practice the land became private property and was passed down from father to son. The great landowners owed allegiance to the king but they were in a good position to defy or ignore him. They possessed an armed force, on which the king could call, but that force could be used against the king or make it difficult for a king to bring them under control. They lived in castles and could defend themselves against rivals and their overlord.

At this time there was a change in the nature of armed force. In the ancient world of Greece and Rome, foot soldiers were the core of armies; now mounted men were central. The stirrup, an invention that came into Europe from the east, made a man on horseback far more formidable. A man in a saddle with his feet in stirrups was more securely on his horse; it was much harder for a foot soldier to knock him off, and the mounted man could combine his power and weight with that of the horse so that they operated as a single unit. A man on horseback riding at full gallop with a lance was a very powerful war machine. The mounted men were known as knights or they were knights in training, who were called squires. The great landowners—the lords—would supply so many knights for the king's service.

Personal oaths of allegiance bound a lord to the king. The lord gave his allegiance by kneeling down and raising his clasped hands; the king would put his hands around them and the lord would promise to be the king's man, to serve him. After the allegiance was sworn, the subject stood and subject and king, both standing, kissed each other. So this was a ritual of both subservience and equality, which signaled the nature of the relationship: The subject promised to be loyal so long as the king protected him. At the beginning of kingship in Western Europe, there was an implicit contract between ruler and ruled, an idea that never altogether died.

The hands being held together is the position we know for prayer, but Christians at first prayed standing, with arms outstretched and facing toward the east, from where Christ was to return in glory. Our position for prayer imitates the ritual of giving allegiance to one's earthly lord. There is argument about the origins of this ritual and the relationship it signified: Was it German or Roman? In Roman society, even in its great days, a young man wanting to move up in the world needed a patron, and as the empire weakened, more and more people began looking for a strongman to protect them. But the ritual itself of hands and kissing was German—the bond created by warriors and their chief.

The oath of allegiance. From the Dresden Sachsenspiegel manuscript (lit. Saxon Mirror), composed between 1220 and 1235.

The concept of the state apart from the people who ran it disappeared. When the king died, all the great subjects had to swear allegiance to the new king. Only then did the territory acquire a new government. Since government was a personal bond, the king could divide his territory among his children as King Lear did in Shakespeare's play and as Charlemagne did in real life, despite all his effort in putting his empire together. New governments were then created by a new round of swearing allegiance. The continuity lay in the bloodline, not in the land of the kingdom. A Roman emperor would not have thought that he could parcel out his empire to his children. His obligation was to hold the empire together. When the empire was divided into west and east, it was done so that its administration and defense could be improved.

The feudal monarchs, because they were so weak, were obliged to seek advice from the powerful people in their country. They did not have an army fully under their control or a regular system of taxation or a civil service. So before they made decisions, they called the important people together to hear their advice and gain their consent. This system of taking advice was formalized when the three estates of clergy, nobility, and commoners met in parliament.

"Estate" did not mean landed estate; estate in the Middle Ages meant a group of people. These feudal societies thought of themselves as three groups of people: the clergy, whose duty it was to pray; the nobility, whose duty it was to fight; and the commoners, that is, everyone else who did the work of society, the money-making and the laboring. "Estates" are very different from classes. Classes have a common relationship with the economy, but these three groups—clergy, nobility, and commoners—were identified by function: praying, fighting, and working. There was a huge difference within them as to their wealth and the tasks they performed within the economy. The clergy could and did include very rich archbishops and bishops as well as the local parish priest, who was a very poor man indeed. The nobility included the great wealthy landowners of the country and also impoverished nobles.

The commoners included the great merchants and bankers, very wealthy people, wealthier than some nobles, and who were the employers of other commoners. It was the wealthy and property-owning commoners who sent representatives to parliament, not the workers and laborers, who were semi-slave serfs.

In France, there were three houses of parliament, which was known as the Estates General. There were the representatives of the clergy in one, the nobility in another, and the representatives of the commoners in the third. In England, the clergy, who were represented by the archbishops and bishops, and the nobility met together in the House of Lords; the commoners had their House of Commons. These names survive in the modern British parliament that, along with the monarchy, is a holdover from medieval times. Britain is now a democracy but it became so by allowing everyone to vote for the House of Commons, limiting the power of the Lords and turning the monarch into a figurehead. It is not a democracy that would be recognizable to democratic Athens in the classical age.

The medieval parliaments were not a regular part of government; they were brought together when the monarch especially needed them. Passing laws was not their chief business; they were called together when the monarch needed extra revenue. From a very low base, kings gradually built up their own power. They had the revenues from their own lands and taxes they could regularly collect; but when costs grew, chiefly because of war, they needed to levy special taxation, so parliament was called together to approve it. The parliament then had the opportunity to air grievances, and some new laws would be passed, initiated by either the king's ministers or the members of parliament.

As towns grew in the Middle Ages, a different form of political organization developed. The towns were governed by councilors who were elected, and they in turn elected a mayor. The medieval monarchs were so weak that when towns developed they did not try to govern them directly; they allowed the towns to govern themselves in return for their allegiance and the payment of taxes and levies. The town council was a gathering of equals, and the oath they took was to each other. This was very different from a world of lords and subjects, which operated everywhere else. The mayor and council, both elected, ruling their own city within a kingdom, is a European invention. Strong monarchs don't allow rival power centers to develop; they put their own men in charge of cities. In Europe, as merchants, bankers, and manufacturers increased their wealth, they were more powerful because of their semi-independent status. In their battle to control the great lords of the countryside, monarchs came to rely on them and their wealth (which they tapped by tax or borrowing). That too was a most unusual development.

	MILITARY ORGANIZATION	POLITICAL CONTEXT	FORM OF GREETING
CLASSICAL	Citizen-soldiers	500 BC Greek democracy Roman Republic	Republican salute
	Paid foot soldiers	27 BC Augustus, first Roman Emperor	Republican salute
	Paid foreign foot soldiers	313 AD Diocletian, Constantine 476 Fall of Rome	Prone
MEDIEVAL	Mounted knights (part time)	Feudal monarchs with "estates"	Kneel Kiss
		Town government of business equals	Mutual Oath

Weak monarchs had clashed with their nobles and contested with their parliaments; in modern times, from around 1400, the monarchs began to get the upper hand. Feudal monarchs were turning into what are known as absolute monarchs: They no longer had to rely on their parliaments. They did not actually abolish the parliaments; they simply did not bother to call them any more. They had found new ways of raising money. The French kings sold public offices; if you wanted to be the collector of customs, you paid the king a large sum of money up front that you then recouped by the fees you charged the merchants. The Spanish kings had the windfall profit of gold from the New World—from Mexico and Peru.

"Absolute" can be a misleading term. It did not mean that European monarchs could do as they liked. They were not tyrants; they had to uphold the law in regular cases and see that justice was done to their subjects, although, when the safety of the state was in question, they had their own more summary courts to deal with difficult customers. They promoted the idea that kings were God's agents on earth and had to be obeyed, which was a larger claim than the early kings had made, but they too were constrained by this formula because they knew they would be judged by God for how they ruled. Certainly they were grander and more remote than the feudal monarchs. The ritual of mutual kissing between king and subject no longer operated: You knelt before the monarch, who might extend his hand to allow you to kiss it.

Monarchs used their funds to buy themselves their own armies. This was now an army of foot soldiers. In the late Middle Ages, new weapons were developed that could knock knights off their horses; these were the longbow and the pike. England developed the longbow, a more powerful weapon than the crossbow, and with it English archers could pierce the armor of mounted men and knock them off their horses. The French at first thought this a dishonorable weapon and refused to be cowed by it. Like the troops charging machine guns in World War I, the French knights charged the archers and were mown down. It did not take long for the French monarch to acquire his own archers. The Swiss developed the pike, which was a long heavy lance: You marched with it over your shoulder and then in battle a square of infantrymen lowered their pikes and pointed them outward so that attacking horsemen would be knocked off their horses or the horses would be speared by the pikes.

Once they had their own armies, monarchs could use them against their own subjects—against great lords who defied the king or poor peasants who refused to pay their taxes. The arrival of gunpowder in Europe in the late Middle Ages helped the king control his great subjects. His army could fire cannonballs at castle walls and destroy them.

Europe had returned to normal: Governments were truly in charge, but its odd beginning of rulers being subject to the ruled was still influential, for in England the parliament survived and strengthened, and a French monarch was forced to revive the Estates General after it had not been summoned for 175 years.

On mainland Europe, since monarchs were regularly at war with each other, kings had strong claims to develop armies. But to defend England the monarch needed a navy more than an army, and a navy could not be used to control the king's domestic enemies. In England, a king wanting to keep a large standing army was regarded as a threat to English liberties. This made it harder for English kings to gain a force that could, if needed, be turned on their subjects. Nevertheless, in the seventeenth century, English monarchs tried to become absolute monarchs on European lines.

THE KINGS WHO MADE THIS ATTEMPT came from the Stuart line, whose origins were in Scotland. When Queen Elizabeth, the Virgin Queen, died in 1603 the throne passed to James VI of Scotland who became, in addition, James I of England. All his Stuart successors ruled over the two kingdoms.

James I, his son Charles I, and his grandsons Charles II and James II, all quarreled with their parliaments. They were frequently ham-fisted in dealing with them, but they did face a real problem. They needed more revenue, but when they sought more taxation from parliament it demanded a greater control over the king's policy. The king naturally enough resisted the parliament's intrusion and the kings tried to find other ways to get money so they would not have to come back to parliament. That of course made the parliament more suspicious, as the king looked like he might be able to do what the monarchs in Europe were doing: bypassing the parliament altogether. But what inflamed these conflicts to the point where men were ready to risk their lives for parliament's cause was religion. The Stuart kings were either Catholic, married to Catholics, or not Protestant enough for their Protestant subjects.

England became a Protestant country during the Reformation but in the German way, where the Reformation began. There was not a Luther in England. England made its first step toward Protestantism by an action of a king, Henry VIII. He is famous as the king with six wives. His first wife was Catholic, but she could not do what was most required of her: produce a male heir. The usual solution to this difficulty would have been for the pope to find reasons to annul the marriage, but the pope had his own reasons for not wanting to offend the queen's family, who were the rulers of Spain. So Henry declared in 1534 that he himself, and not the pope, was head of the Catholic church in England. He appointed an archbishop who would annul his marriage to Catherine and marry him to Anne Boleyn. After him, the Church of England, as it was now called, became steadily more Protestant, but it still kept some Catholic ritual and it still had bishops and archbishops. This upset the zealous Protestants—the Puritans—who wanted a thorough reformation of the church.

JAMES I
|
CHARLES I (*executed 1649*)
|
Cromwell interregnum
|

CHARLES II (*became Roman Catholic on deathbed*) JAMES II (*openly Catholic; excluded 1688*)

James I resisted the demands of the Puritans, but he did great service in agreeing to a new translation of the Bible. The King James version, elegant yet sprightly, was the Bible of the English for the next three centuries. Charles I, James's son, preferred in theology and ritual what is now known as High Anglicanism, which for most Protestants and not just the Puritans was far too close to Rome. Charles caused great offense by forcing his views on the Church of England, which was the official established church, of which he was head. He was not Catholic but his queen was, with special arrangements for her to have her own priest who said mass at court.

Charles soon came to an impasse with his parliaments and for eleven years ruled without them, which he was entitled to do because parliament only met at the king's command. With care he might have found ways to avoid calling parliament ever again, but very stupidly he attempted to impose his preferred mode of worship on the people of his other kingdom, Scotland, who were more Protestant and more fiery. The Scots launched an army into England to force Charles to desist. In order to fight the Scots, Charles needed an army and so was forced to call a parliament to levy the taxation to pay for it. Parliament now had its chance and moved to limit the king's powers over church and state and increase its own. It executed Charles's chief minister and his High Anglican Archbishop of Canterbury. Charles was initially at parliament's mercy, but eventually he gathered a royalist party to support him, and parliamentarians and royalists went to war. Parliament won the war and its chief general, Oliver Cromwell, organized the trial and execution of the king in 1649. Cromwell then ruled in the king's place; he called parliaments and quarreled with them, and while he lived, England was in effect a military dictatorship. When he died, one of his generals reconvened the parliament of Charles's time and it invited Charles's son to return from exile and take the throne.

Charles II began his reign with no formal changes to the powers of king and parliament, though the execution of his father was a sharp reminder not to push his claims too far. He was sympathetic to Catholicism and became a Catholic on his deathbed. He had no children by his queen, though many by his mistresses. The next king would be his brother, James, who was openly Catholic. Parliaments tried to pass laws excluding him from the throne, to which the king responded by dismissing the parliaments. But without parliament he could not raise taxes. He overcame this difficulty by secretly receiving funds from the absolutist king of France, Louis XIV, who, in order to make France completely Catholic, withdrew the toleration that had been granted to Protestants. Thousands fled to other countries. Protestantism in France was under attack at the very moment, 1685, that Protestant England acquired in James II a Catholic king.

James, despite knowing that he was not wanted, did not proceed carefully. He openly promoted Catholicism, which he took to be the true faith. After all the trouble of the English Civil War and the military dictatorship that followed it, many parliamentarians were prepared to put up with James, but then his queen, his second, Catholic wife, produced a male heir. England appeared to be having a line of Catholic kings. As soon as that happened, nearly the entire parliament determined to be rid of him. The parliamentary leaders secretly invited a Protestant ruler to come with his army to England and take the throne. This was the Dutchman, William of Orange, who was married to Mary, a daughter of James by his first, Protestant wife. William was a champion of the Protestant cause in Europe and fought battles to protect his country from Louis XIV.

Parliament's treason went very smoothly. The wind blew favorably, and William had a quick passage across the English Channel. As soon as he landed, nearly all James's troops deserted him and went over to the enemy. James fled to Ireland, which was very convenient because parliament did not have to try him or chop off his head. It simply declared that the throne was vacant and installed William and Mary as joint monarchs.

The powers of king and parliament were now redefined by the parliament, and only on these terms did it grant the throne to William and Mary. The document that rewrote the constitution was called the Bill of Rights. It is a mixture of the rights of parliament and the rights of individuals:

Rights of individuals

Every subject has the right to petition the monarch [James had punished churchmen who had petitioned him against his religious policy].

No excessive bail should be required, nor excessive fines imposed.

No cruel or unusual punishments should be inflicted.

Protestants should have the right to bear arms.

Juries should not be stacked by the crown.

By modern standards this is a limited list of individual rights, but this was the foundation document for all subsequent statements of rights. The United States's Bill of Rights even includes the very term "cruel and unusual punishments."

Rights of parliaments

Parliament must be called regularly.

The king cannot suspend laws or fail to implement them [James had done both with regard to the laws against Catholics].

Only parliament can approve taxation [James, like his predecessors, had taxed on the basis of his royal authority].

No standing army can be kept in time of peace without parliament's consent [James had created an army].

The king cannot set up his own courts [James had set up courts to enforce his control of the church].

The king and his ministers should not interfere in the election of members of parliament [James had attempted to organize the election of a parliament sympathetic to his views].

Members of parliament should be able to speak freely in parliament without threat of legal action [what is now called parliamentary privilege].

Parliament had thus made itself into a permanent part of the constitution. And all without any blood being spilled. This coup by parliament gained the name "The Glorious Revolution." The monarch was still left with considerable power: to choose ministers, to direct policy, to make treaties, and to declare war. But since monarchs could only get revenue with the consent of parliament, they had to choose ministers who had support in parliament. Over time, this constraint led to the system that operates in Britain today and in all the countries that have followed the Westminster style of government: The monarch or their representative is officially in charge, but in all matters they are obliged to follow the advice of ministers responsible to parliament.

William and Mary had no children. Anne, Mary's sister and James II's daughter, ruled after them and she had no children who lived. Parliament then determined who should be the next monarch. It passed over many Catholic descendants of the Stuart line who had strong claims and chose Sophia, the Electress of Hanover in Germany, a granddaughter of James I, who was a Protestant. She and her heirs would be the new royal line. The parliament had organized to get the sort of monarch it wanted. By the time Anne died, Sophia too was dead, so the crown passed to her son George, who did not speak English and who spent much of his time in Hanover.

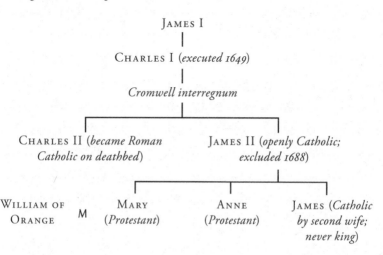

JAMES I

|

CHARLES I (*executed 1649*)

|

Cromwell interregnum

CHARLES II (*became Roman Catholic on deathbed*)   JAMES II (*openly Catholic; excluded 1688*)

WILLIAM OF ORANGE **M** MARY (*Protestant*)   ANNE (*Protestant*)   JAMES (*Catholic by second wife; never king*)

In setting these arrangements in place, parliament made two important provisions, which are still part of the English constitution:

> The monarch must be a Protestant, a member of the
>   Church of England, and not be married to a Catholic.
> The monarch appoints judges but they can be removed only
>   by a vote of both Houses of Parliament.

The Bill of Rights ensured that parliament—the legislature—was a strong, permanent, and independent part of the system of government. The independence of the judges was now secured from the executive—the king and his ministers—who appointed them. The state was fixed as Protestant, which was seen as a guarantee of its freedoms. Protestantism in its beginning was an endorsement of individual freedom because it was a defiance of the authority of popes and bishops and an elevation of individual conscience and experience. In England, it was the more firmly attached to freedom because the enemies of England—the absolutist monarchs of France and Spain—were Catholic, and the English kings who attempted to bypass parliament were either Catholic or seen to be soft on Catholicism. Preserving parliament and preserving the Protestant faith became the same cause.

In these ways, the aristocracy and landed gentlemen of England, who composed its parliament, established the institutional arrangements of a liberal state. It was not totally liberal because it was based on hostility to Catholics. Nor was it reached by the embracing of liberal principles. Parliament always declared it was merely preserving its ancient rights and liberties. It was during long battles with kings that parliamentarians had worked out what was necessary to checkmate any king who had a mind to operate like the absolute monarchs on the continent: He must call parliament; he can't tax without it; he mustn't control the courts. The broader principles became clear after the victory was won.

The philosopher who formulated the liberal principles to support the parliamentary coup was the Englishman John Locke.

His book *Two Treatises of Government* was published in 1690, just after the revolution. Locke argued, drawing on the Roman idea of natural law, that men have certain natural rights to life, liberty, and property, and that in forming governments they make a contract: They confer power on governments so that their rights can be protected. But if these rights are not protected, then the people have the right to dismiss this government and form another. The godlike character of kings, the obligation of subjects to obey—all this was swept aside and government made into a businesslike transaction. But the philosopher was not the first to make government a contract: This had been implicit in the relationship between feudal monarchs and their subjects, and while parliament continued to exist, even if only in men's heads, the notion of ruling with subjects and not against them survived. In England, Locke's book justified what had happened in the past and was no longer revolutionary; to American and French rebels later, it gave the justification for revolt and the language of rights by which they defined their new order.

THE FRENCH REVOLUTION in its early days had as its aim the creation of a constitutional monarchy like England's. The reformers got their chance because in the 1780s the monarch was close to bankrupt. Louis XVI employed reforming finance ministers who planned to make the ramshackle taxation system uniform, fairer, and more efficient. The most spectacular change was that the nobility was, for the first time, to pay tax at the same rate as everyone else. They had previously paid less on the grounds that they contributed to the state by providing themselves and their men to fight for it. This was no longer how the monarch acquired his armed force, but of course the nobility opposed the tax-reform measure. The absolute monarchs had sidelined the nobility in order to create a state that they controlled, but they had not eliminated them. Nobles had enormous prestige and held important positions in the law courts (that had to register royal decrees), at the king's court, and in the army. They raised a storm of protest at being asked to pay taxes at a higher rate and strangely won a lot of popular support for this resistance to a "tyrannical" attack on an ancient right—which shows how limited royal absolutism was. A bolder, more determined monarch than Louis might have pressed on and enforced the change; instead, he accepted the advice from all quarters that only with the authority of parliament could a new taxation scheme be introduced. So after a gap of 175 years, the Estates General was summoned.

Immediately, a fierce argument broke out over how it was to meet. The three orders or estates each had their own house of parliament: clergy, nobility, and commons (or Third Estate, as it was known in France). Before any measure was adopted, all three houses had to agree to it. The leaders of the Third Estate, chiefly lawyers, knew their chance of giving France a new constitution would be slim if they had to get agreement from the nobles and clergy. They demanded that the three houses meet and vote together and that as recognition of the Third Estate's number, industry, and wealth it should have double the number of representatives. The king at first refused any change to the old manner of meeting; then he half yielded and, as was the way with Louis, made matters worse. He agreed to double the representation of the Third Estate, but the houses were still to meet separately. So long as they did that, of course, it made no difference how many representatives the Third Estate had; whatever they proposed could be vetoed by the nobility or clergy.

The argument continued when the Estates General met in 1789. The Third Estate declared itself to be the true National Assembly and invited the other orders to join it. One day, when they arrived at their meeting place in the royal palace at Versailles, they found the doors shut. The doors were only shut because the room was to be painted, but the delegates were so jumpy, fearing that the king was going to close them down, that they went immediately to a nearby indoor tennis court and there swore oaths not to disband until they

Sketch by Jacques-Louis David, *Tennis Court Oath*, 1791.

had given France a constitution. There is a drawing by the royal artist David of this moment, which is a famous case of life following art. Five years earlier, David had painted *The Oath of the Horatii*, which shows the Horatius father and his sons with arms raised in the republican salute. The same salute was used by the revolutionaries of the Third Estate as they vowed to give France a constitution.

Many of the clergy and a few of the nobles did join the National Assembly. The king indicated that he would give the Estates General a permanent place in the constitution, but he would not consent to the three estates meeting together. He threatened violence to the assembly if it did not return to being one house in three—but when met with defiance, he did not resort to it. The king backed down and very weakly told the other orders to join the Third Estate.

The leaders of the assembly were men of the Enlightenment; they had very clear liberal and egalitarian principles. Their slogan was liberty, equality, and fraternity. The assembly issued its manifesto under the title *Declaration of the Rights of Man and of the Citizen*; these were rights not just for the French, they were rights for all mankind. These are, in summary form, its chief articles:

Men are born and remain free and equal in rights.

These rights are liberty, property, security, and resistance to oppression.

Sovereignty resides in the nation.

Liberty consists in the freedom to do everything which injures no one else.

Every citizen has a right to participate personally or through a representative in making the law.

No person shall be accused, arrested, or imprisoned except by process of law, which shall provide only punishments that are strictly necessary.

No one shall be disturbed on account of his opinions, including his religious views.

Every citizen may speak, write, and print with freedom but will be responsible for abuses of this freedom as defined by law.

A constitution without the separation of powers is no constitution at all.

It is a glorious document, the founding document of modern democracy, but it was bound to produce an inglorious revolution. The men who endorsed these principles wanted a constitutional monarchy like England's, but what security did a king have when sovereignty had been proclaimed as residing with the nation and all men had been declared equal? The framers of the document wanted to rule, and they decided, when they came to draw up a constitution, that only property holders should vote. But how could they exclude the common people when they had been declared to be equal? It was only by the action of the common people that Louis was forced into the pretence of accepting the declaration; they had stormed the royal fortress of the Bastille and forced the king to leave his palace at Versailles and live in the midst of the people in Paris. The common people, having helped make the revolution, were not going to go away.

Too much had been promised and threatened for France to produce a constitution like England's or a bloodless revolution like

1688. That revolution had not worked on new principles; now there was an overabundance of new principles. The king soon made clear that he did not accept the principles and would undo any changes to his rule if he could. That gave the radicals their chance. They insisted that they had to make alliance with the people and control or remove the king in order to make any change secure. That bred a reaction in those who wanted change, but not democratic change with the people in charge.

The revolutionaries were soon fighting among themselves. One reason why David never turned his drawing of the Tennis Court Oath into a painting was that a number of the people who had been present had been executed as enemies of the revolution. The

	MILITARY ORGANIZATION	POLITICAL CONTEXT	FORM OF GREETING
CLASSICAL	Citizen-soldiers	500 BC Greek democracy Roman Republic	Republican salute
	Paid foot soldiers	27 BC Augustus, first Roman Emperor	Republican salute
	Paid foreign foot soldiers	Diocletian, Constantine, Late empire 476 Fall of Rome	Prone
MEDIEVAL	Mounted knights (part-time)	Feudal monarchs with "estates"	Kneel Kiss
		Town government of business equals	Mutual Oath
MODERN	Paid foot soldiers	Absolute monarchs (England: parliamentary government)	Kiss hand
	Citizen-soldiers (conscripts)	1789 French Revolution	Republican salute

radicals adopted the name the Jacobins, since they met in a former convent of the Dominicans (Jacobins); their leader was the cold, steely Maximilien Robespierre. The Jacobins turned themselves into a revolutionary dictatorship. They executed the king, expelled their opponents from the assembly and closed down their newspapers, and set up special kangaroo courts to execute traitors to the revolution. They had this much excuse for a dictatorship: France was in mortal danger because the revolutionaries had courted war with the monarchies of Europe in order to force them to adopt the principles of the Rights of Man. The army they created for this purpose was of a new sort, a conscription of all the manhood of the nation—the people in arms.

Portrait of Mirabeau, leader of the French Revolution in its early stages. Beside him sits a bust of Brutus, and on the wall behind him is David's painting of Brutus, when his executed sons are brought home.

The revolutionaries had read their Livy. The patron saint of revolutionary tyranny was Brutus, the founder of the Roman Republic, who agreed to the execution of his own sons. There was a bust of Brutus in the assembly beside the podium. Streets were renamed Brutus; parents called their children Brutus. Since the Jacobins had created a republic, there could no longer be playing cards depicting kings, queens, and jacks. Instead, there were sages, virtues, and warriors. Brutus was one of the sages. The king was referred to as Tarquin and, as in Rome, it was an offense to call for the restoration of the monarchy. That implacable republican virtue—the belief that everything should be sacrificed for the state—the willingness to see blood flow and to think it was purifying: This was the Roman contribution to the first modern, totalitarian state.

CHAPTER 6

Emperors and Popes

OUR HISTORY BEGINS WITH A GREAT empire and then with its collapse. Europe took much from the Roman Empire and was profoundly shaped by the nature of that collapse. *The Decline and Fall of the Roman Empire*, the title of Edward Gibbon's great history, is etched into our consciousness. What must it have felt like to live after that event, to know there had been a great civilization and now it was gone? But if you were to ask a medieval lord or scholar what it was like to live now that the Roman Empire was no more, they would have been puzzled. In their eyes the Roman Empire still survived. There was, in fact, something called the Roman Empire existing into the nineteenth century. The last Roman emperor traced his line back to Augustus. How was this so?

The reign of Augustus began in 27 BC and in the west the empire he founded lasted for 500 years. Around AD 400 the empire was permanently divided into east and west, and the Eastern Empire survived another thousand years, until 1453. The barbarians who invaded the western Roman Empire acknowledged the emperor of the Eastern Empire. Clovis, the first Christian king of the Franks, received the title "Consul" from the emperor in the east. The pope, who survived in Rome, also acknowledged the eastern emperor, and in the pontiff's eyes, despite all the barbarian invasions and the collapse of the empire in the west, the key parts of the old order were still intact. There was a pope in Rome and there was an emperor, a Christian Roman emperor, who now resided in Constantinople. Those two authorities, the pope and the emperor, would jointly control Christendom. But when the pope really needed the eastern emperor's help, the emperor couldn't do much to save him.

The danger to the pope came from the Lombards, who were a second wave of German invaders in the eighth century. They were poised to make a complete takeover of Italy, including Rome and the lands around it. This represented a great threat to the pope. Even today, the pope still has his own individual plot of ground, Vatican City. It is tiny but it is his own state; he is not part of Italy. The popes have always feared that their independence would disappear if they were not sovereign in their own territory. Imagine if the Vatican were just part of Italy. Italy might pass a law saying there should be equal opportunity in all spheres of life, including the church. The church would be investigated for never having appointed a female bishop, let alone a pope. The church's wealth might be taxed by the Italian state. Italy might pass a law saying there should be condoms in all public toilets.

The pope in the eighth century, likewise, did not want to become subject to the control of the Lombards. He sought help from the eastern emperor, but he was too busy dealing with the Muslim invasions of his territory. So the pope looked north across the Alps to the Franks, the Germans who had made the strongest state in the west, in what is now France. King Pepin, the Christian Frankish king, went south into Italy and subdued the Lombards. He made sure that the pope was left with a large belt of territory around Rome, which was to be his. With many changes of boundaries, this territory survived as the pope's until the nineteenth century. It was only then, with the creation of a unified Italian state, that the pope was confined to the small kingdom he has today.

King Pepin's son was Charles the Great, or Charlemagne. He greatly expanded the territory of the Frankish kingdom. His lands extended across the Pyrenees into Spain; halfway down Italy, including the land his father had allotted to the pope; in the east to Austria and well into modern Germany. Since the fall of Rome, there has been no single European state that was so extensive except for the short-lived empires of Hitler and Napoleon. In Germany, Charlemagne was dealing with the Saxons, who had not

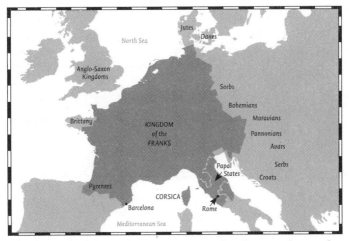

The kingdom of the Franks grew to cover modern France and parts of Germany, Spain, and Italy.

crossed into the Roman Empire. They were pagans; he gave them the option of converting to Christianity or being made into slaves and shipped back to his heartland.

In the year 800, Charlemagne visited Rome and attended mass on Christmas Day in the cathedral. After the mass, and seemingly with no prior warning, the pope placed a crown on Charlemagne's head and declared him to be Roman emperor. He made his own emperor in order to have a power that would protect him. But since he was turning his back on the emperor in the east, he needed to have an excuse for what he was doing. What could be easier! A woman had become emperor in Constantinople; she had blinded her son, who was the emperor, got rid of him and put herself on the throne. By the pope's deed, she was no longer emperor over the west.

There was later great dispute between popes and emperors about what had happened in the cathedral on Christmas Day, 800. Popes emphasized that it was the pope who put the crown on Charlemagne's head, which indicated that the pope was superior to the emperor. But after the pope put the crown on Charlemagne's head, he bowed to Charlemagne. Emperors said that the pope was thus acknowledging the superior power of the emperor. Emperors reasonably said that the pope was only able to choose this protector because Charlemagne had made himself a strong figure in his own right. His strength hadn't depended on the pope's assistance.

Charlemagne's empire was very different from the Roman one, and Charlemagne was a very different ruler from a Roman emperor. He was basically still a barbarian king. He was educating himself; he had learned to read—that is, he could read Latin—but he had difficulty writing. Until the end of his life, he kept a little wax tablet beside his bed in order to practice his writing, but he never really got the knack of it. But he did have a clear understanding of empire as a civilizing force, something he learned from the Roman example. His German ancestors had lived by plunder, and it was the desire for more plunder that took them into the Roman Empire. Governments can be organized so that they are just a system of plunder, to enrich those in power and their friends. There are ancient and modern governments like this. Saint Augustine, who lived in the last days of the Roman Empire in the west, wrote in his *City of God*: "If there is no justice, what are kingdoms but great robberies?" Charlemagne knew of this work and understood this point; Saint Augustine was one of his favorite authors. With the pagan Saxons in the east, he could be savage and cruel until they converted to Christianity. But once they were Christians within his realm, he took it upon himself to make sure that they were ruled justly.

Charlemagne, though poorly educated himself, encouraged education and became the patron of educated men, who were ordered to find and copy the ancient manuscripts. Nearly all the Latin works that have survived were copied in Charlemagne's time. Without him, the classical inheritance would have been very slim.

Charlemagne faced huge handicaps. He had no bureaucracy; communications were poor; there was little trade; towns were tiny; there was a great amount of chaos. In all of this, his empire was most unlike the Roman. His mode of government was to appoint counts and dukes throughout his realm to keep the local lords in order and to ensure that they gave their allegiance to Charlemagne. There was no institutional base to this empire; its government depended on the personal power of its leader.

Charlemagne built his palace at Aachen, close to the present border between Germany and Belgium, and in his time close to the center of his realm. Only the chapel survives. It is built in the Romanesque style, that is, after the style of Rome, with the rounded arches. The pillars supporting the arches were actually Roman; Charlemagne brought them back from Italy.

After building up this huge empire with such great effort, Charlemagne decided in the customary German way that after his death it should be subdivided among his sons. But only one son of his survived, so the division of the empire occurred at the next generation, among his grandchildren. The grandsons fought among themselves and Charlemagne's empire fell into three parts. The western part eventually became modern-day France; the eastern part became the basis of Germany. But in the fights among his grandchildren and in the chaos of the Norse invasions, Charlemagne's methods of control disappeared. The counts and dukes established themselves as local strongmen with only very weak allegiance to whoever might be king. Europe had reverted to what it was immediately after the fall of Rome: Power was very much dispersed, and before there could be strong kingdoms again, kings would have to subdue counts and dukes.

With the disappearance of Charlemagne's empire, the pope had lost his strongman to protect him. For a while, he made do with whatever local princes he could find and crowned them emperor. Then, in 962, a new, strong king, Otto the First, emerged in the German part of Charlemagne's old empire. The pope crowned him as Roman emperor and, thereafter, whoever became the king of Germany was, after being crowned by the pope, also Roman emperor and later Holy Roman Emperor.

The German kings were the only kings in Europe who were elected. The practice of the Germans before they came into the Roman Empire was to run a mixed system of inheritance and election. There was a royal family, whose male members would be the candidates for election. This was to ensure that a good warrior was chosen to be king; the German tribesmen did not want to be saddled with a dud.

It happened that in France for a long time all the kings produced able sons, and so gradually, inheritance became the sole means of determining who was going to be the French king. But in Germany, the kings were not so adept at producing good heirs so the system of election was maintained and continued more strongly when the German king regularly became the Holy Roman Emperor. The emperor had general oversight of all Christendom and election ensured that theoretically any Christian prince could be chosen for the job. In practice it was nearly always a German prince who was chosen. There were at first numerous electors, local strongmen like archbishops and dukes; eventually there were just seven who bore the name "elector."

The German king/emperor struggled like kings everywhere to exert his power over local strongmen, some of whom were his electors. Since the emperor had to curry favor with the electors to win his post, he was sometimes yielding power rather than claiming it from them. The situation was even more complicated because, as well as the local struggles for control, the emperor for centuries was involved in a battle with a figure who rivaled him in power and prestige: the pope.

Pope and emperor had helped build up the power of each other. The emperors had protected the papacy, most importantly by protecting the papal territories. On occasions, they had intervened in Rome to ensure that there was a pious pope and not some adventurer in the chair of Saint Peter. The popes had built up the power of the emperors by crowning them and giving them their title, Roman Emperor. But from the eleventh century the two quarreled because popes began to insist that the church should be run from Rome and kings and princes should not meddle in its affairs.

The Catholic church was the great international institution of the Middle Ages, but it was always being undermined because kings and local power brokers wanted to control who became bishops in their own territory. This was not simply so they would have a voice in church affairs; the bishops had many jobs to bestow—priests and officeholders in the church—and they controlled large portions of land from which the church derived its income. Sometimes, a third of the land was in the church's hands; in Germany it was almost half. Those with secular authority wanted to influence how the bishops wielded their enormous power.

When we say the church was an international body, think of it in this way. Toyota, which is run from Tokyo, is in the business of making cars. Say, in the US, its chief executive is appointed by the president and the plant manager is appointed by the local mayor. Officially, the plant manager and the chief executive owe their allegiance to Tokyo, but of course in practice, since they have been appointed by the president and the mayor, they will always be looking over their shoulder to see that they don't displease them. And the mayor and the president might not have selected people who know anything about cars; they will give these jobs to the people they need to please this week. This is what the medieval church was like: It had been undermined, subverted from within, and plundered by local power brokers and the monarchs of Europe.

The pope, who wanted to upset all those cozy arrangements and bring authority more firmly back to Rome was Gregory VII, who became pope in 1073. He declared that he would in the future appoint bishops. The emperor Henry IV replied that *he* would continue to do so. The emperor stood firm, so the pope excommunicated him; that is, he expelled him from the church. The emperor was no longer able to take mass or to have any of the services that the church provided. This was always a very powerful weapon for popes because having excommunicated a king, they told the people in his territories that they did not have to obey him. In this case, German dukes and princes, who always wanted to escape from the emperor's control, were delighted to find that he was excommunicated and could be ignored.

Henry IV then crossed the Alps in winter and found the pope in a castle at Canossa in northern Italy. He waited outside for two or three days in the snow, begging the pope to see him. He had cast off all his royal regalia; he was dressed in humble clothes. Finally, the pope relented and the emperor knelt before him and asked for forgiveness. The pope lifted the excommunication, to the great annoyance of the German princes. This was very humbling for Henry, of course, but it was also quite a clever ploy. It was very hard for a Christian pope to refuse to grant forgiveness. The emperor did not completely abandon his position. The dispute dragged on for years and finally there was a compromise. The emperor was allowed to have some influence in choosing bishops but it was to be the pope who actually gave them their staff of office and their official robes.

These battles continued between popes and emperors for a long time. They were literally battles. The pope went to war against the emperor. You might ask, how does the pope carry on a war? He is a monarch in his own right; he has his own territories from which he collects taxes that he then uses to hire soldiers. He looks around for allies wherever he can find them. Sometimes, the pope made an alliance with the German princes who did not want to be subject to the emperor and opened a front, as it were, in the emperor's rear. The towns in northern Italy, which in the Middle Ages became the richest towns in Europe, did not like being subject to the emperor, whose realm extended this far south. Sometimes, the towns allied themselves with the pope to fight off the emperor. Often, they played both sides, switching allegiance as was most advantageous.

The pope as warrior is wonderfully described by the Renaissance artist Cellini in his autobiography. Like many Renaissance men, Cellini was multitalented, not only a superb goldsmith, but also good with weaponry. When an enemy was attacking Rome, he was on the battlements with the pope, giving instructions about the firing of the cannon. Among the pope's enemies was an old Spanish officer who had formerly fought for the pope but was now on the other side. He was a long way off, not thinking he was in range at all. He was standing in a very relaxed way with his sword slung in front of him. Cellini gave the order for the cannon to fire. It was a freakish shot; the ball hit the officer's sword, which it pushed back, cutting him in half. Cellini was very distressed at this: killing a man before he had time to prepare himself for death. He knelt before the pope to ask for absolution. But the pope was delighted at his deed. He said, "Yes, I forgive you; I forgive you all the homicides you commit in the service of the church."

Here is a sculpture of Saint Peter, the supposed first bishop of Rome, dressed as a medieval pope, with a gorgeous cloak and great crown. He has not forgotten his humble origins as a fisherman: One of his feet is bare. Most people in medieval times would not have been offended at this grandeur. The pope should be a great prince; he should have all the trappings of royalty because he was the head of the church and had to meet other monarchs as an equal.

Pope and emperor fought each other to a standstill. They never had a complete victory, one or the other. Their dispute was like conflict between bosses and workers. There are strikes and threats of firing, often intense and bitter, but you know there will always be a settlement and that there will always be bosses and workers. The significance of the pope–emperor struggle is that the pope never claimed to be emperor and

Medieval bronze statue of St. Peter enthroned in St. Peter's Basilica, Rome.

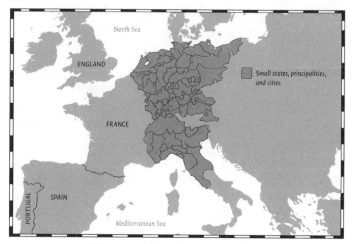

Western and Central Europe in 1648.

the emperor never claimed to be pope. They both acknowledged that the other should exist; they were arguing about their relative powers. This is a very important characteristic of Western Europe, which distinguishes it from the Byzantine Empire in the east. The practice in Constantinople was that the emperor was not only the ruler of the civil affairs of his empire but also of the church. There was a patriarch, but the patriarch was appointed by the emperor and under his control. In the west, the two authorities of church and state were separate and had independent authority. This was a continuing bar to any universal claims by kings.

The effect of the long-term struggle between emperor and pope was that they weakened each other. The long-term effect on Central Europe, running from Germany in the north to Italy in the south, can be seen on the map. Here is a patchwork of small states, principalities, and cities. In the west, England, France, and Spain have now emerged as unified countries. Dukes and counts have been brought under control and the king's writ runs right through his territory. In England, this was much helped by its conquest in 1066 by Duke William, who, in seizing control of all parts of the country by force, established a stronger monarchy than in mainland Europe. In Central Europe, two great powers—emperor and pope—had been struggling, trading away their local authority in order to fight each other. The result was that the smaller units gained power rather than lost it. They were self-governing bodies only marginally affected by their overlords. It was here that two transforming developments of modern (post-1400) Europe occurred: the Renaissance and the Reformation. Why they occurred is a hard question to answer; why they could occur here is easier.

The northern cities of Italy, where the Renaissance began, were small city-states such as the ones that had existed in classical Greece. The Italian cities were rivals, militarily and culturally: They went to war with each other and they wanted to outdo each other with the splendor of their art. Because they were states as well as cities, they concentrated many talented people in one place. The nobility, unlike those in the rest of Europe, did not regard their landed estates as their natural home; they lived in the cities as well. The variety and vitality of city life characterized whole societies. These were the places that could conceive and carry out the project of recreating the ancient world.

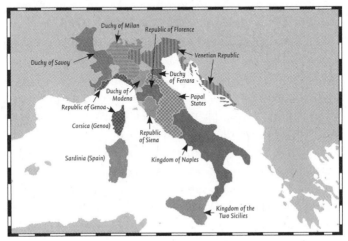

The states of Italy during the Renaissance (c. 1494).

Luther's Reformation took root and flourished in Germany because secular power was dispersed. It was the duty of the emperor to put down Luther's heresy and rather belatedly he attempted to do so. Luther was given safe passage to come before him and the princes of Germany to be examined. When Luther refused to recant, the emperor declared that he was a heretic, that no one should support him, and that he should be arrested. His orders were immediately frustrated by Frederick the Elector of Saxony, who seized Luther and took him into hiding. It was while Luther was hidden in his castle that he began to translate the Bible into German. Frederick and the other German princes who supported Luther saw the advantage of putting themselves in charge of the church and its lands. They increased their own power at the expense of pope and emperor—and so Lutheranism was born.

Germany and Italy remained divided until the second half of the nineteenth century. They came late to national unity and were more prone than the older, unified states to take up the intense nationalism fostered by the Romantic movement. In the twentieth century, they were the two states that adopted nationalism in its most aggressive and exclusionist form, which goes under the name of fascism.

Though in itself the position of emperor carried little power, the Holy Roman Empire survived. From the late Middle Ages, one family always provided the person who was elected Holy Roman Emperor. This was the Habsburgs, one of the great ruling dynasties of Europe. They supplied monarchs for Spain, Austria, parts of Italy, and the Low Countries. To them, holding the position of emperor added to their prestige; their power came from their own kingdoms. Voltaire, the guru of the Enlightenment, mocked the Holy Roman Empire as neither holy, nor Roman, nor an empire, which was true enough, but its survival was always somewhat magical, carrying a name and an idea in a very odd form. It took the head of a new empire to abolish this strange survival of an old one. He was Napoleon Bonaparte, who took charge of France in 1799, ten years after the revolution began.

The revolution began by proclaiming liberty, equality, and fraternity; within four years, there was a Jacobin dictatorship ruling by the guillotine; when it looked like Robespierre was continuing to rule in the same way, even though the war crisis was passed, he was overthrown and executed. Moderate republicans then tried to stabilize the revolution, to keep out the common people and the supporters of a return to monarchy, who had a large and growing following. The government had to use force against both these opponents to survive and lost all credibility. This gave Bonaparte his chance. He had made his name as a general in the revolutionary wars that France had waged against the monarchical powers of Europe. He was a son of the Enlightenment, a believer in the principles of the revolution, except in the right of the people to govern themselves. Since the French had most signally failed at that task since 1789, Bonaparte's approach was very attractive. He was the most seductive of dictators. He wanted no group to enjoy special privileges; all citizens were to be treated as equals; all children were to have the chance of education provided by the state; all positions were to be open to people of ability. He gathered men of great talent into his government, ignoring altogether what part they had played during the revolution, whether as monarchists or republicans, supporters of the Jacobin terror or its opponents. He gave them the task of giving France an orderly, rational system of government.

One reason among several for not giving too much weight to the "absolutism" of the French monarchs was that, although they had built up their own power, they still ruled over a patchwork rather than a unified state. There were different systems of law and administration and a myriad of special privileges, exemptions, and concessions, all of which the monarch had made to secure new areas for France and new allegiance to himself. The revolutionaries swept all this aside; their aim was a unified nation. But during the chaos created by fighting each other, they did not get far in establishing a new regime. That was the task Napoleon set himself and his panel of experts. Their greatest work was the development of the Civil Code,

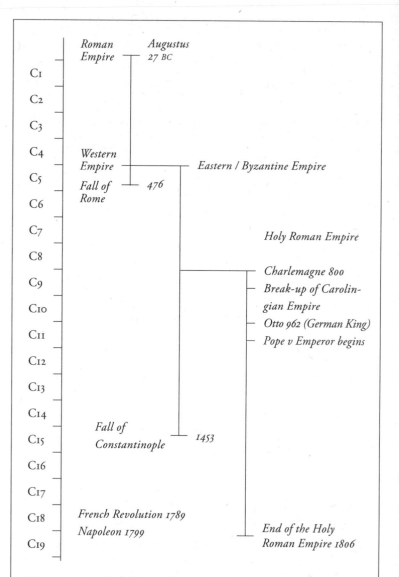

C1	Roman Empire	Augustus 27 BC
C2		
C3		
C4	Western Empire	Eastern / Byzantine Empire
C5	Fall of Rome	476
C6		
C7		Holy Roman Empire
C8		
C9		Charlemagne 800
C10		Break-up of Carolin-gian Empire
C11		Otto 962 (German King)
C12		Pope v Emperor begins
C13		
C14		
C15	Fall of Constantinople	1453
C16		
C17		
C18	French Revolution 1789	
C19	Napoleon 1799	End of the Holy Roman Empire 1806

The continuity of the Roman Empire. Holy Roman Emperors traced their lineage back to Charlemagne, then through the Byzantine emperors and through to the first Roman Empire and Augustus.

an imitation of the great code of Emperor Justinian, a single document in which the law on every subject was laid down.

The Roman example was important to Napoleon. At first, he called himself Consul, then Emperor; but like Augustus, he did not mean by that title to obliterate the republican status of France. Like the Romans, he planned to create an extensive empire where the principles of republican France would be the basis for a just and orderly society. He continued the wars with the great powers of Europe that the early revolutionaries had begun and won amazing victories. He extended the boundaries of France, and beyond France he reshaped principalities and kingdoms and put his brothers in charge of them. Right across the continent he swept away medieval rights, privileges, and anomalies and established his new rational order. When the powers of Europe finally managed to cooperate for long enough to defeat Napoleon, much of his work could not be undone. What pleased him most, reflecting on his life in exile on Saint Helena in the South Atlantic, was the survival throughout Europe of his Napoleonic Code—which still survives. What did not survive was the Holy Roman Empire. Napoleon abolished it in 1806 when he regrouped several small states in Germany into the Confederation of the Rhine.

Arch of Constantine, Rome: commemorating his victory over a rival emperor in AD 312.

Arc de Triomphe, Paris: commissioned by Napoleon at the height of his power in 1806.

Napoleon was a nonbeliever, in God that is; he was a great believer in chance and destiny. But he realized how firmly people were attached to their faith and how useful religion was in maintaining morality and good order. The early revolutionaries, as children of the Enlightenment, did not have this respect for organized religion. Nothing did more to divide French society and alienate people from the revolution than its attack on the Catholic church. The revolutionaries seized church land and set up a rival national church, which the pope refused to recognize. Napoleon was determined to end the bitterness and divisiveness that this had caused. He reached an agreement with the pope, a Concordat, which acknowledged that the Catholic faith was the religion of the great majority of the French people. Not *all* the French people, and Napoleon would not agree to the pope's demand to withdraw freedom of religion, which allowed Protestants and others to practice their faith without impediment. On the appointment of bishops the Concordat reinstated an old practice: The state would nominate bishops and the pope would invest them.

The pope was present in Notre Dame cathedral when Napoleon was crowned emperor. He anointed Napoleon and his empress, Josephine; he blessed the imperial regalia: orb, hand of justice, sword, and scepter. But Napoleon himself put the crown on his own head. It was a replica of the crown the pope had placed on Charlemagne, a light, open crown, like the laurel wreath that Romans gave to their victors.

Languages

T HERE WERE TWO UNIVERSAL languages in the Roman Empire: Latin in the west and Greek in the east. Greek, though in a somewhat different form, is still spoken—in Greece itself and by Greeks settled around the eastern Mediterranean and in the wider Greek diaspora. No territory on Earth now has Latin as its common language. Latin is regularly described as a dead language; if that is so, it has been an unusually lively corpse.

Latin was at first spoken only by the people in Rome and the small tract of country around Rome. It expanded as Roman rule expanded, and after hundreds of years, it was being spoken throughout the western empire. The division between the Latin west and the Greek east ran through what is now Serbia. So Latin became the language of a good part of the Balkans, all of Italy, France, and Spain, but not of Britain. Though the Romans went to Britain, the Celtic language of the Britons survived. Everywhere else in the west, the local languages gradually disappeared and the people took up Latin.

Rome itself sensibly did not have a language policy, which is the most self-defeating act of public policy. It is extremely hard to suppress a language and install another in its place. No one in the ancient world would have contemplated it. Rome was an inclusive empire in that it allowed the leaders of the societies it had conquered to remain leaders and to become part of the Roman elite, to become generals and even emperors. Eventually, in 212, all peoples in the empire were declared to be citizens and, hence, protected by the law. So it is a tribute to the Roman Empire that after three or four hundred years, the local languages disappeared.

Latin was the language of administration, of law, of the army, of trade, and it eventually had a quiet victory.

The Latin spoken in the further reaches of the empire was not formal Latin, the Latin of scholars, lawyers, and politicians, the Latin you learn at school or at a university. It was the Latin spoken by soldiers, local administrators, and traders, and even before the empire broke up there were regional variations. The Latin being spoken in Italy could well have been different from the Latin spoken in France. Once the empire broke up, Latin evolved into a number of separate languages, which are known as Romance languages, that is, languages in the manner of the Romans, just as Romanesque architecture is descended from Roman forms of architecture.

The chief Romance languages are French, Italian, and Spanish. Consider the word for horse in each: In French it is *cheval*, in Spanish *caballo*, in Italian *cavallo*. There is no sign here of the Latin word for horse, which was *equus*. In English we have *horse*, which comes from the German, but we also have *equestrian*, a horse rider or matters to do with horses, which comes from *equus*. Often, the Latin words in our language are more formal words. From *horse* we have *horsey*; we might say someone is a horsey person, but it is more polite to say an equestrian or someone interested in equestrian events. In Latin, there was a slang word for a horse, *caballus*, something like a nag, and it is from that word that the Romance words for horse come: *cheval* (French), *caballo* (Spanish), *cavallo* (Italian). The Spanish and Italian forms in this case are much closer to the original than the French.

The French are very careful about their language. The French Academy deliberates on what English words they will allow into the language: Is T-shirt or bulldozer acceptable? And will it be *la T-shirt* or *le T-shirt*, depending on whether T-shirt is to be masculine or feminine (something that English does not bother with)? It would not be wise to point out to the French that the language they are protecting is a debased form of Latin.

Latin is a highly inflected language, that is, the meaning a word has in a sentence depends on the ending of the word (its inflection). The Latin word for year is *annus* (from which we get *annually*, slightly more formal than *yearly*). The Latin word for master or lord is *dominus*. If we want to say in Latin *in the year of our lord*, the endings of *annus* and *dominus* change to *anno domini*. *Anno* means *in the year*; *domini* means *of the lord*. It is from *anno domini* that we get the abbreviation AD in calendars that count years from the birth of Jesus Christ. Because it is an inflected language, Latin does not have to call on words like *in* or *of*. There are just two words, *anno domini*, for our six words, *in the year of the lord*, which is one reason why Latin is good for mottos—because it is so succinct. You do not have little fussy words in between the main words. Nor does Latin need a definite article *the* or an indefinite article *an*. *Annus* means *the year* or *a year*.

The order of the words in a Latin sentence does not matter. *Domini anno* still means *in the year of the lord*. In English if you switch word order you change the meaning or get no meaning: *In the lord of the year* or *of the lord in the year*.

Latin did have words for *in*, *at*, and *of*, which you could use for emphasis. But as Latin was spoken by people who were not quite clear about all the rules, they would increasingly use the words for *in*, *at*, and *of* and not worry about changing the word endings. Gradually Latin moved from a language where endings changed to one where prepositions—*in*, *at*, *of*—were regularly used and the word stayed the same. This explains why Romance languages do not inflect their nouns, and hence, word order is crucial.

In Latin, there was no word for *the* but if you wanted to speak emphatically you could say "I want to buy *that* apple" or "Give me *that* peach." The word for *that* was *ille* or *illa*, depending whether the noun it preceded was masculine or feminine. The amateur speakers of Latin used *ille* or *illa* more and more and again didn't worry about changing the word endings. Then *ille* and *illa* were shortened in French to become *le* and *la*, which have to be placed before every

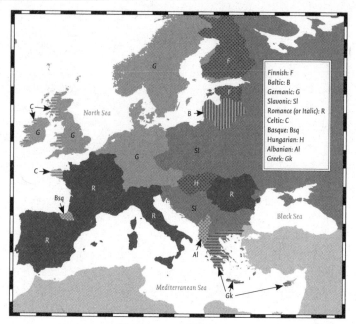

The languages of Europe.

noun. In Spanish, the shortening produced *el* and *la*; in Italian *il* and *la*. Think of all the shouting and pointing by the amateur Latin speakers that gave the Romance languages their definite article.

In the fifth century, Germans invaded what is now France, Spain, and Italy, and yet these people speak a language derived from Latin. How can this be so? It is time to look at the language map of Europe. Most of the languages spoken are part of a larger language family, either Romance, Germanic, or Slavonic. A few countries are loners that have a language not closely connected to any other. Such are the Greeks, the Albanians, the Hungarians, and the Finns.

In Western Europe, Germanic languages prevail in the north and Romance in the south. Two countries are mixed: Belgium has a Germanic language in the north and a Romance language in the south. In Switzerland, a Germanic language is spoken in the north and Romance in the two southern corners. In addition to these minor Romance languages, we must now include Portuguese alongside the big three (French, Spanish, and Italian) and, a surprise, in Eastern Europe, Romanian. That country lies to the north of the River Danube, which was usually the border of the Roman Empire. The Romans extended their control north of the river in a great bulge for a hundred years, but that would not seem a long enough exposure to Latin for it to have become the base for Romanian. This has led to the suggestion that the Romanians lived south of the river, where they had a long exposure to Latin, and later moved north, not a suggestion that the Romanians are happy with.

In most of Central and Eastern Europe, the languages are Slavonic: in Poland, the Czech Republic, Slovakia, Bulgaria, and the former Yugoslavia. This introduces the Slavs, who lived beyond the Germans and who invaded the Eastern Roman Empire in the sixth and seventh centuries and settled in the Balkans. Some of the Slavs remained in areas that had never been part of the empire: Poland, the Czech Republic, and Slovakia. After they settled in Europe, the Slavs were Christianized: the Poles from the west, so they became Roman Catholic; most of the people in the Balkans from Constantinople, so they became Greek Orthodox.

Latin (and its Romance offshoots), Greek, and the Slavonic and Germanic languages are all descended from a common origin, a language that has been given the name Indo-European. Linguists attempt to construct some of its elements by working back from the commonalities in the languages it spawned. They argue about where the Indo-Europeans were located—somewhere to the east. They had a word for snow; their word for sea seemed to relate to an inland sea. The language is *Indo*-European because the Indian language Sanskrit and Iranian are also descended from it.

The discovery or the construction of this language only happened in the eighteenth century. Until then, the study of languages in Europe had assumed that they were all descended from Hebrew, because that was the language the Jews spoke, and by implication, it was the language of Adam and Eve, the first people. Hebrew is a different language altogether from European languages—it is not descended from Indo-European—and so the pursuit of Hebraic origins was a complete dead end. But in the era of Enlightenment in the eighteenth century, scholars could throw off the Biblical framework and develop new theories. The breakthrough was made by William Jones, an English judge residing in India. He noticed similarities in the basic vocabulary of Sanskrit and European languages—the words for numbers, parts of the body, and family members. Here are the words for brother:

Brother (English)
Bhratar (Sanskrit)
Broeder (Dutch)
Bruder (German)
Phrater (Greek)
Brat (Russian)
Brathair (Irish)

Jones judged that these similarities were more than accidental and surmised that these languages had a common ancestor that no longer existed. So the reconstruction of Indo-European began.

Two European countries—Hungary and Finland—have languages that are not descended from Indo-European. The two languages are related. Their speakers arrived in two separate movements from Asia. The Finns arrived in prehistoric times; the Hungarians were latecomers, horsemen marauding widely in the ninth and tenth centuries at the same time that the Norsemen came plundering from the sea. They were persuaded to settle in the Danube Valley and they became Christian.

The previous map displays the language distribution at present. It would not have looked very different immediately after the Slav and German invasions. The German invasion of the Roman Empire led to some change in language distribution but, as we have seen, Latin in its Romance form survived in France, Italy, and Spain. The extent of the change can be seen on the next map, which more closely displays the present-day boundary between Germanic and Romance languages. The boundary of the Roman Empire was the Rhine river. What the map displays is how far across the Rhine the Germanic languages advanced. Not very far, as you see.

It is a puzzle to know why the new language boundary took the form it did. In Belgium, the line that divides the language groups is in open countryside. There are no natural features, a river or a mountain range. You are driving along a straight road; the village to your right will speak a Romance language (Walloon) and the village to your left a Germanic language (Flemish). This language boundary has not changed in 1,500 years. There is a suggestion that there might have been a Roman defensive line running straight west to east, a barrier to keep the Germans who were already across the Rhine from going further. It might have stopped them here, but obviously the Germans got around it further east.

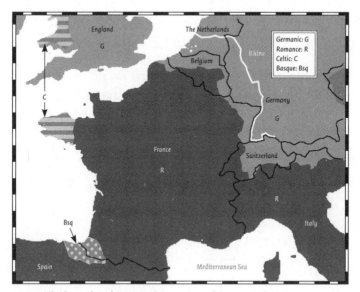

The boundary between Germanic and Romance languages.

Broadly speaking, you can see that the strip of territory between the Rhine and the language border is roughly 50–100 miles wide until it narrows in the mountain country to the south. In this territory the German settlement was dense enough for the Germanic language to supplant Latin or incipient Romance. The Germans went right through Western Europe, into Spain, across into north Africa. But in all those places, the language remained Latin/Romance, which indicates much less dense German settlement than in the borderlands.

When France expanded as the great power of the seventeenth and eighteenth centuries, it pushed its boundaries north and east but the language map didn't change. The people in the eastern border country of France are still German-speaking. In the north of the country near the Atlantic coast, the people speak the Germanic language Flemish. The map shows there are some other areas of France where French is not spoken. In the southwest near the Spanish border, there are Basque-speaking people who claim independence from both France and Spain. Basque is not an Indo-European language; no one quite knows where it comes from. On the western peninsula of Britanny, the Breton language is a Celtic survival. When the Angles, Saxons, and Jutes invaded Britain, some of the Britons in England crossed the Channel to Brittany and the people here still speak Breton, though the area of Breton-speakers is contracting.

As they advanced into France, the Germans no longer supplanted Latin/Romance, but they contributed some German words to the evolving language, particularly those concerned with kings and government and with the feudal system; that is, the terminology of the new ruling class. The words for shame and pride in French come from the German, very important concepts to the German warriors.

It is in England that the Germanic languages had a complete victory, which is to be expected, given the overrunning of the native Britons by the invading Angles, Saxons, and Jutes. Then, in the ninth and tenth centuries, there was a second invasion of

England by people speaking a Germanic language, the Norsemen, or Danes. The basic vocabulary and grammar of English emerged with the melding of these Germanic tongues. In the process, English lost the inflections of its German origins.

In 1066, there was a third invasion of England, this time by the Norman French, led by Duke William. The Normans were originally Norsemen from the north encouraged to settle in France by the king to put a stop to their marauding. They spoke their own version of French, which, being a Romance language, still carried a lot of Latin. England's new ruling class continued to speak Norman French for several centuries until this too was melded into English, which resulted in a huge increase in the vocabulary of English. There were now two or more words for almost everything. To the English *king* and *kingly* were added *royal*, *regal*, and *sovereign*. English has a vocabulary several times larger than German and French—it is, after all, an amalgam of German and French.

Here is a table summarizing the evolution of languages in Western Europe and England after the fall of the Roman Empire.

	WESTERN EUROPE	ENGLAND
C5: *German invasion*	• *Germanic language advances 100 miles across the Rhine* • *Latin becomes Romance*	• *Germanic language completely replaces Celtic language*
C9: *Viking invasion*	• *Settlements in northern France* • *Germanic Norse added to Romance to become Norman French*	• *Settlements in eastern England* • *Germanic Norse added to Germanic Anglo-Saxon to become English*
1066: *Norman invasion of England*	• *Norman French spoken by England's rulers*	• *French (and Latin) added to English*

Latin had disappeared as the language of ordinary people but it survived as the language of learning, literature, and the church. This is why so many Latin words passed into all European languages. Since churchmen and scholars were still speaking and writing Latin, it was a living language, and hence, subject to change—or, by purist standards, it was being degraded. There was a chance that even in these circles Latin would go the way of Romance. The first restoration job on Latin was undertaken at Charlemagne's direction. The old Latin manuscripts were copied and efforts made to make the current use of Latin match the classical original.

Since Latin was the language of learning and literature, learning and literature became extremely remote. If you wanted to be educated, you had first to learn a foreign language. In the Middle Ages, the majority of the people were illiterate, which is common enough. What is most unusual is that the rich and powerful were also illiterate because they did not know Latin. So oral culture of song and story ran right through society. The jester or the minstrel kept the lord in his castle amused; there was no chance that the lord could retire with a book. Tradition and custom were all-important because so little of the world could be understood and managed by writing. When European nobles and knights arrived in the Holy Land on crusade, the Muslim gentlemen were astounded that they were so crude and unlettered.

Gradually, a literature in the vernacular language emerged; that is, it was written in the first language of all the people and not in Latin. The first stories in France were called *romans*, after the language in which they were written. It was a way of dismissing them—it's a trashy local work—it's a *roman*. *Roman* then became the French word for story. Because the stories were about knights, their heroic deeds and their love for beautiful maidens, the subject of the stories was identified as Romance. This explains the odd double meaning of Romance, as a language derived from Latin and the subject treated in trashy novels.

The second great restoration job on Latin was undertaken in the Renaissance. Scholars despised the Middle Ages because, among other things, the Latin was so degraded and impure. Their aim was to write in the Latin of the great classical authors. Petrarch, the pioneer scholar of the Renaissance, scoured Europe searching for a copy of Cicero's letters. When he found them he composed, in perfect Latin, a letter to Cicero himself. Noblemen and gentlemen were now being educated—and in Latin, not because it was the language of the church and theological dispute, but so that they could read the classics and write in the Latin of the classical age. Until the twentieth century, Latin was at the center of secondary and tertiary education. I myself had to pass Latin in order to enroll in college. University graduation ceremonies were conducted in Latin and the terminology of degrees is still frequently in Latin: *ad eundem gradum* to the same degree, *cum laude* with honors (praise), *summa cum laude* with highest honors, and *honoris causa* by reason of honor (for honorary degrees).

Latin was a great bond between educated men across Europe (girls did not study Latin). It gave them a common second language, a social bond, and a sort of code they could drop into. In the English House of Commons, a speaker would quote a famous classical saying in the Latin and not translate it. If you did not understand it, you should not be there. Sexual terms that could not appear in print could be printed in Latin so that ordinary people could not understand them and be corrupted. So just when a book got interesting it turned foreign. English still bears the marks of this—*genitalia* for sex organs is Latin; so is *pudenda*, a wonderful example of Latin succinctness and of puritanical attitudes to sex: It too refers to the sex organs, particularly women's, and means literally "matters that are shameful."

At the same time as the Renaissance revival of Latin, the vernacular languages gained new status and respect—first, because of the invention of printing in the 1450s. The first books to be printed were the classical authors, but the demand for them was limited. Printers gained a wider market when they issued books in the local language or translations of the classics. Shakespeare, who it is said had little Latin and less Greek, learned his classical history from North's translation of Plutarch's *Lives of the Noble Grecians and Romans*, which appeared in 1579, when Shakespeare was fifteen. That gave him the material for *Julius Caesar* and *Antony and Cleopatra*. Second, the Protestant reformers of the sixteenth century wanted the people to read the Bible for themselves, so it had to be translated into the local language. Luther's first task was to translate the Bible into German. For Protestants, Latin ceased to be the language of holy things.

Original books continued to be written in Latin and so were immediately accessible to educated men throughout Europe. Copernicus, who first posited the sun at the center of the universe; Kepler, who formulated laws of the planets' motion; and Newton, who completed the Scientific Revolution, all wrote in Latin. But after the seventeenth century, scientists and philosophers wrote in their local language and their works had to be translated to reach a wider audience.

There was one late flowering of Latin that still survives, the system for naming plants that was developed by the Swedish botanist Linnaeus in the eighteenth century. He had learned Latin at school and read in Latin Aristotle's works classifying the natural order. His system gives in Latin two names to plants: their genus and their species. Discoverers of plants are rendered into a Latin form if they are to be part of the plant's name. Joseph Banks, who was the botanist on Cook's great voyage, is immortalized in the name Banksia, the shrubby Australian plant with bottlebrush flowers.

When Christianity began, the universal language in the west was Latin. It became the language for the governing of the church, for the arguments over its doctrines, for the pronouncements of the faith, and for the conduct of church services. It was not like Arabic, a holy language, which was the language of the prophet

Muhammad. Jesus spoke in Aramaic and his words were recorded in the common Greek of the eastern Mediterranean. The language of the Old Testament was Hebrew. But Latin brought all the faithful together and it continued to be the language of Catholic worship until the Second Vatican Council (1962–65) authorized the use of the local language. The encyclicals of the pope continued to be issued in Latin. Pope Paul VI declared the church's teaching on contraception and abortion in *Humanae Vitae* (1968; *Of Human Life*). Some of the faithful continued church services in Latin, almost as an underground rite. The previous pope, Benedict XVI, was more favorably inclined to the use of Latin in the mass, but in 2021, Pope Francis reimposed Benedict's restrictions on celebrating the mass in Latin.

Like the idea of the Roman Empire, Latin has been a long time dying.

CHAPTER 8

The Common People

You WILL LIKE the common people. They are dirty, smelly, and not attractive to look at because they are undernourished, worn down, and marked by disease, battered, and scarred by hard work in all weathers. Why would you like them? Because their fortunes are easy to follow; they go on doing the same thing century after century. Nearly all of them grow food.

We don't need a timeline to discuss them; we have a graph that shows very little variation. The graph shows the proportion of people who are growing food or who are very closely connected to it; that is, we include people living in rural villages or settlements and supporting farming, such as wheelwrights, blacksmiths, and laborers. The figures are very crude estimates. In the Roman Empire, roughly 90 percent of the people were in the countryside. There were great cities in the empire, preeminently Rome itself, but they constituted only 10 percent of the population. The big cities were supplied with grain from the country, but grain

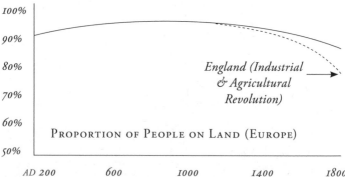

is a heavy product and could not be carted far by land before its whole value was consumed. The grain for Rome came from Egypt by sea, which was by far the cheapest mode of transport. In the later stages of the Roman Empire, the government subsidized the distribution of grain in Rome to keep the people content; Rome was like a third world city of today, a great magnet but unable to provide a living for all the people who flocked to it. Along with free bread, Rome provided regular spectacles in the Colosseum. The Roman satirist Juvenal described the government surviving by "bread and circuses."

This grain trade was exceptional. Most of the trade in the empire was in light, valuable luxury goods that could afford high delivery costs. In the Roman Empire, as in Europe until the nineteenth century, most people survived on what was grown or made nearby: Their food, drink, clothes, and shelter were all local products. Old cottages in Europe have thatched roofs not because it is more picturesque than slate but because it was the cheap material on hand. So in the economy, the Romans were not a transforming force; their innovation lay in binding an empire together by a single law and with a military organization that was outstandingly efficient. The straight Roman roads, parts of which survive, were designed by army engineers for the prime purpose of allowing soldiers to march quickly from place to place. That's why they are straight; if they had been designed for horse and carts, the gradients would have been more gentle.

In the last two centuries of the Roman Empire, the cities were losing population as the German invaders attacked them; trade contracted and local self-sufficiency became more imperative. In its great days, the empire's cities did not have walls. The enemies of Rome were kept out at the frontiers. In the third century, walls around towns began to be built, and in places the evidence for the decline of towns is that later walls enclosed a smaller area. By the disappearance of the empire in AD 476, the proportion of people in the countryside had risen to 95 percent.

It remained there for centuries. The German invasions were followed by others: Muslims in the seventh and eighth centuries, who raided into southern France and into Italy; Vikings in the ninth and tenth centuries, who spread great mayhem. Peace came in the eleventh and twelfth centuries, and trade and town life began to revive. Some towns had almost completely disappeared after the fifth century; others had been much reduced.

The graph begins a very slow fall. In the fifteenth century, Europe started to expand overseas, which led to a growth of commerce, banking, and shipping, and hence, the growth of towns. By 1800, the proportion of people in the countryside in Western Europe might have fallen to 85 percent, slightly lower than in the Roman Empire. There was very little movement over such a long time. The one exception is England, where by 1800 the rural proportion was falling rapidly as cities boomed; by 1850, half the population of England was in cities.

The people growing food differed in status; at any one time and over time they might be small proprietors, slaves, ex-slaves, serfs, ex-serfs, tenants, sharecroppers, and laborers. We will call them all peasants. But the work was the same whoever you were and whatever the era. In Italy, southern France, and Spain, plowing in the nineteenth century was the same as in Roman times. The plow was primitive; think of the plow as a forked stick with a cutting blade at its base. An oxen or horse pulls the plow; the plowman holds and directs it, and the blade penetrates not very far below the surface. It was not much more than scratching the surface. You plowed in checkerboard fashion, along the field and then across it.

One of the great inventions of the early Middle Ages was the wheeled plow. The inventor is unknown. This was more effective for the heavier soils of northern France, Germany, and England. In principle, it was the same as modern plows except that it was pulled by animals and held to the job by humans. There was a sharp blade that cut the soil and a moldboard that lifted and turned the soil that had been cut. This produced furrows, not just scratches, and

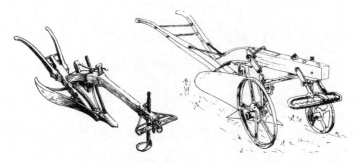

The early forked plow was relatively light, scratching the surface of the soil in small square plots. The heavier wheeled plow was able to turn the deeper soils of Northern Europe, creating ridges and furrows in long strips called "furlongs."

the furrows all ran the same way, parallel to each other—not the crosshatching of the old plow. In the heavy soil, water could run off down the furrows. Plowing was hard work; you were not just steering the plow. If you didn't hold it firm with your shoulders and your arms, it would fall over rather than cut the soil. After you plowed the land, you broadcast the seed, which was easier work. You walked over the fields casting the seed in swaths to fall onto the ground. Then the seed was covered with a harrow, a sort of rake.

Men plowed. Men, women, and children harvested, and since the time for a safe harvest was short, people would be recruited from the towns and the local soldiers might be turned out of the barracks to help. Harvesting was done with the sickle, a curved blade with a handle. Archaeologists find them in the most ancient human settlements. They were still the standard harvesting mechanism in Europe up until the early twentieth century. The communist revolution in Russia in 1917 wanted its new flag to honor the workers; it carried the hammer and sickle, the hammer for urban workers and the sickle for country workers.

You must not think of cultivation and harvest as you see it now with farmers sitting in air-conditioned tractors driving over the land. Peasants were plodding, bending, and straining over every inch of ground year after year.

Harvesting scenes from a German manuscript, Speculum Virginum, around 1200.

After the stalks of wheat or barley had been gathered, the grain had to be beaten out of the ears. The tool to do this was a flail, which had a long wooden handle to which a flat board was attached with a leather thong. You swung the handle and brought the board down flat on the ears lying on the floor of the barn. The doors of the barn were open and the breeze would carry away the chaff and leave only the good grain on the barn floor.

The grain was made into flour and then into bread. Bread was the staff of life. You eat hunks of it and not much else; you do not eat meat regularly. You might have some butter or cheese to go with your bread. Bread is the meal; it is not on a side plate or a couple of slices in a nice basket. It's three or four hunks. You eat about two pounds of it a day if you are well-off. That's a large loaf per day. Grain was grown everywhere, even in places where it was not well suited and where today grain would not be grown. Because transport was very difficult, the grain had to be grown close to where it was consumed. Grain that came from elsewhere was very expensive. Grain could be moved by sea, but inland for any distance only became possible in the eighteenth century with the building of canals.

Everyone was always anxious about the harvest. The talk about the weather was not making conversation; it was a people pondering their fate. If the grain did not ripen or bad weather spoiled the grain before it could be harvested, then the whole community would suffer. Grain would have to come from elsewhere and it would be very expensive. In times of shortage of grain, the price of bread doubled or tripled. This is not like one item in the supermarket that costs a lot more and you have to eat something else for a time. This is the cost of your whole food intake that is doubling or tripling. Once it does that, you are hungry or maybe you are starving.

But peasants were growing the food, so wouldn't high prices benefit them? Only for those with large holdings. If you grew only enough to feed your family with little to sell, a failure in the harvest would mean you didn't have enough to feed yourselves and you would have to buy extra. Some had small plots that, even in good times, were not enough to supply their family; they relied on getting extra work on larger properties and buying extra food. Many were laborers with no land of their own; if they lived with their employer and got fed, they would not be so badly off; if they lived in their own cottage, they would be regular buyers of bread. People in the towns, of course, were always buyers. There were lots of people in deep trouble when the price of grain went up.

As soon as there was a grain shortage, owners of grain—those who grew it in a big way and dealt in it—were tempted to hold it back so that the price would go even higher, or to send it off somewhere else if the price there had risen further and leave the locals without any grain. As soon as governments were halfway competent, roughly from 1400 onward, they attempted to control this business. They passed laws to prohibit hoarding and the transporting of grain out of localities where there was scarcity. If the magistrates did not enforce these laws, the people could enforce the laws themselves. They went searching for hoards of grain and forced large farmers to sell. They attacked wagons or boats that were carrying grain elsewhere. It was partly because of the potential for riot and disorder that governments were forced to become involved.

Most people most of the time were living with uncertainty over food. Luxury is to eat well regularly; fat is beautiful; holidays are feast days. We still have a pathetic remnant of this in our society in the celebration of Thanksgiving or Christmas Day, that is, when we are expected to mark the day by eating a lot—even though we eat well all the time. I try to preserve something of the proper ethos of a feast day by never eating turkey on any other day.

The 85–95 percent of the people who worked the land made civilization possible. If peasants had grown only enough food for themselves, there could not have been any cities or lords, priests or kings, or armies—who all depended on others growing their food. Whether they wanted to or not, the peasants had to supply food to other people. This process can be seen most clearly in the serfs of the early Middle Ages passing a portion of their crop over to their lord as rent, some to the church as a tithe, as well as working on the lord's land without pay so that he would have his own crop. Later, the obligation to work ceased and payment to the lord and priest was in money.

In the early Middle Ages, there was no taxation by the state; before, in the Roman Empire, and afterward in the emerging states of Europe, peasants were taxpayers. We have a depiction of tax-collecting in the Roman Empire showing the tax collectors and the peasants coming to pay. The transaction is recorded not on paper

Peasants paying tax to collectors during the Roman Empire (note the record book on the left). This relief, found on the Rhine frontier, is from about AD 200.

but on waxed boards. This is the key transaction for the running of the empire: You take money from peasants and you use it to pay your soldiers. Screwing money out of peasants is the foundation of civilization. You see how direct this tax-gathering is. You do not write to this taxman or send him a check; he doesn't deduct a portion of your pay as you earn it. The taxman is a live person who seeks you out; if you refuse to pay, he will return with the force to make you. Tax-paying was not bureaucratically controlled; it was a face-to-face encounter. In the Roman Empire, the tax-gatherers were called *publicani*, that is, those who are collecting for the public. They were hated. Even Jesus assisted in stereotyping them as the worst people when he said there is no particular virtue in loving those who love you—even the tax-gatherers will do that. In the King James version of the Bible, *publicani* is translated as publicans. Jesus is criticized for mixing with "publicans and sinners." This was very unfair to those who held licenses for public houses.

To speak of peasants being screwed is, of course, very loaded language. Perhaps they should have enjoyed paying their taxes, or at least only grumbled about it; no one likes paying taxes, but we get the benefit of the services that government provides. Except the peasants got no services. Governments did not run schools or health systems. Mostly they didn't look after the roads; roads were matters for local concern, except where they had a military importance. The Romans looked after the public health of their cities by providing water and sewerage systems, but they did not do anything for the countryside. Until very recent times, most tax collected, 80 or 90 percent of it, was spent on the armed forces. So did the peasant benefit from the foreign foe being kept at bay? Not really, because war to the peasant meant battles fought over his land, and his food and animals being taken to feed both armies.

The threat of force and the insistence by their betters that they were inferior people who were bound to obey and comply kept peasants paying their taxes, but still there were regular protests, riots, and rebellions. Peasants were inspired to act by their own view of the world, which was that if kings, bishops, and landlords left us alone we would be perfectly all right. It was easy to think this because peasants did grow all their own food, build their own housing, brew their own beer, and weave their own clothes. A lot of modern people choose to drop out of the rat race; they think all you need to live is a plot of land on which to grow your own food. You do not have to be on the land for long to realize that you actually need money to buy jeans, drugs, liquor, DVDs, and gas, and phone bills have to be paid. Soon the dropouts are taking part-time work and neglecting their farming; soon after that, they are back in full-time work. But for the peasants, self-sufficiency was real; to them, the government and the church were mere burdens and the money taken from them was robbery.

THE PEASANT REVOLTS were always suppressed—until the first year of the French Revolution. The French peasants, like all the others, had been serfs in the Middle Ages. When serfdom came to an end in Western Europe in the late Middle Ages, a variety of situations were available for the ex-serfs. In France, the law said the peasants were the owners of their lands, which they could sell and leave. However, they and whoever bought the land still had to pay the old feudal dues and obligations to the lord, such as giving something when the lord's daughter got married or being obliged to work on the lord's land so many days a week. These had been turned from gifts and service into money payments. So these peasant owners of land still had to pay an assortment of rents. Owner *and* tenant: It was a most unusual situation.

The owners of the large estates—it could be a lord but now also a rich, middle-class person—employed smart lawyers to check back through the records to see that all dues and obligations were being met by some money payment. When the dues and obligations were changed into money, no account had been taken of inflation; the money payments were not, to use our term, indexed for inflation. So the lord had every incentive to find obligations that had been overlooked or wrongly calculated. There could scarcely be a more annoying and aggravating relationship; the lord had seen the ownership of the land pass to the peasant and he compensated for that loss by ratcheting up the money payments for the old dues and obligations. The peasants fought back; they banded together to hire their own lawyers to do battle with their lord's.

When the king called the Estates General in 1788, the peasants assumed that a new day was going to dawn; all these hated impositions would be lifted from them. But there was a troubling delay; they heard about the fall of the Bastille and the king's acceptance of the National Assembly, but their payments to the lord survived. Some foul conspiracy must be afoot. The price of bread was high and rising because the last harvest had been poor and the new harvest was not yet in. Rumors swept the countryside that aristocrats and bandits were trying to stop the reform from reaching the country. Peasants actually marched out to meet and defeat the bandits. They also marched on the lords' châteaus and demanded that the lord or his agent destroy the great registers in which their payments were recorded. If the lord agreed they went away satisfied; if he did not they set the château on fire.

The revolutionaries in Paris did not know what to do about this peasant rebellion sweeping the countryside. This is not what they expected at all. In due time, once they had formulated the Rights of Man and a new constitution, they would address the peasant grievances. The difficulty was that among the revolutionaries themselves were people who received payments from peasants on lands they had bought.

The revolutionaries did not want the king to send out his army to control the peasants, which was the normal response to peasant rebellion. If the king ordered the army out he might, after dealing with the peasants, turn it on the revolutionaries. So the leaders of the assembly decided that they must do what the peasants wanted. On the evening of August 4, 1789, in an all-night session, speakers denounced the dues and obligations. Men who had benefited from them outdid each other in condemnation and promise of reform. It was half stage-managed and half hysteria. But they did not lose their heads completely: A distinction was to be drawn between payments that related to personal service, which would be swept away immediately, and those that related to property, which would be removed later and with compensation to owners. It was very hard to make this distinction; the peasants refused to draw it and from that moment never again made payments of any sort. In 1793, when the revolution became more radical and a new constitution was created, all dues and obligations were canceled.

The peasants became full owners of their land, entirely free of their landlords. They then became a conservative force in French politics throughout the nineteenth century, compared to radical working-class people in the cities, who attacked private property and wanted to create a socialist society. The big men in France could always rely on the peasants to vote that down. They held on to their small plots, which meant that agriculture in France would remain small-scale and inefficient. Today, the peasants benefit from European subsidies, which means they can market their produce at lower prices and compete against larger and more efficient farmers. The French peasants are now screwing us!

In England, a totally different arrangement of the land followed the end of serfdom. Feudal dues and obligations in any form disappeared. The serf became a tenant farmer in the modern way, simply paying rent to the landlord. The tenant held a lease, sometimes for long time, perhaps even for life, but when the lease expired the landlord could remove the tenant and rent the land to someone else. In France, the peasant had greater security; he could not be removed but he had to pay the feudal dues and obligations. The existence of a modern, commercial relationship between landlord and tenant in England allowed for the huge jump in agricultural productivity that is called the Agricultural Revolution.

The revolution had two elements: an improvement in agricultural practice and a rearrangement of land holdings. It had nothing to do with the improvement of agricultural machinery; tractors and harvesting equipment came much later.

First, as to agricultural practice. The basic problem faced by all cultivators is that regular cultivation exhausts the soil. How do you solve it? The German farmers outside the Roman Empire simply moved to new land when the old land was exhausted. This is only semipermanent agriculture. Within the Roman Empire, the land on a farm was divided into two. One part was cropped; the other lay fallow, which means the land was rested; horses, oxen, sheep, and cattle grazed on it, eating the stubble of last year's crop and dropping their manure. At the end of the year, the fallow was plowed up and a new crop sown, and the other part of the farm reverted to fallow. This remained the system in Southern Europe until the nineteenth century. In Northern Europe in the Middle Ages, a three-field system developed, two carrying crops and the third lying fallow. One grain crop was planted in autumn, the other in spring. You see what an increase in efficiency this is: Two-thirds of the land is producing grain instead of one half.

In England in the eighteenth century, farms were divided into four and crops planted in each of them. This was the Agricultural Revolution. How might this work? If the land is always cropped it will become exhausted. The clever lateral thinking behind this technique was that two of the crops were grain, as before, and two were fodder for animals, such as turnips or clover. They take different elements out of the soil and so the soil was not exhausted by continuous grain cropping. Clover actually regenerates the land by fixing nitrogen from the atmosphere into the soil. Since crops were being grown for animals, who were previously left to survive in the fallow, more cattle and sheep could be run; they ate better, became larger, dropped more manure. At the end of the year, a cattle or sheep field became a grain field and yielded a better crop. More and better animals and better crops: This was the outcome of the new four-field practice.

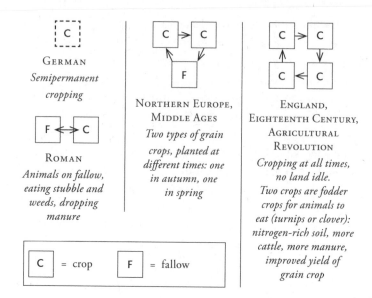

GERMAN
Semipermanent cropping

ROMAN
Animals on fallow, eating stubble and weeds, dropping manure

NORTHERN EUROPE, MIDDLE AGES
Two types of grain crops, planted at different times: one in autumn, one in spring

ENGLAND, EIGHTEENTH CENTURY, AGRICULTURAL REVOLUTION
Cropping at all times, no land idle. Two crops are fodder crops for animals to eat (turnips or clover): nitrogen-rich soil, more cattle, more manure, improved yield of grain crop

C = crop   F = fallow

At the same time, landholdings were rearranged so that each farmer had a consolidated holding—his own farm—with clear boundaries. This replaced the medieval system in which a farmer had a strip or a portion of each of the three large common fields into which the village land was divided. You did not have your own farm; the farm was the village's, though its ownership lay with the lord. The village made decisions about what was to be planted, where, and when, and everyone's cattle grazed on the fallow ground. Outside the three common fields was waste ground, marsh or woodland, also available to everyone for grazing or for collecting thatch and firewood.

The rearrangement of the land into consolidated holdings was carried out by act of parliament, a special act for each village. The parliament of England was a congress of the great landholders, who had decided that consolidation (or enclosure, as it was known) was necessary for the new agricultural practices to be properly followed. Cultivation of the new crops and the better care of animals needed individual attention, not common control by the village.

A landlord who wanted to increase the yield of his lands and so increase the money he could charge in rent could make the adoption of the new practices a requirement for holding a lease to a consolidated farm. A farmer who refused to grow turnips would be thrown out; that is, his lease would not be renewed.

The consolidation was carefully done. Commissioners examined everyone in the village to establish what their existing rights were. The right to farm so many strips in the common fields and the right to graze on the common lands was translated into the right to a consolidated holding of a certain size. The people who suffered from the rearrangement were cottagers who had the right only to graze on the common lands; they received a small plot that was no good for anything. These were the people most likely to leave for the cities. But overall, the new agricultural practices on consolidated holdings required more labor, not less. There was a general exodus to the cities but this was because the population was growing rapidly.

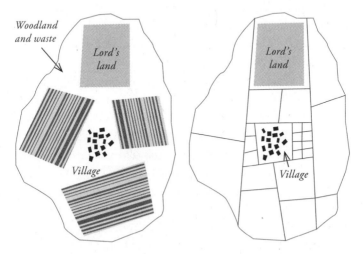

Woodland and waste

Lord's land

Village

Lord's land

Village

BEFORE ENCLOSURE
Three fields divided into strips

AFTER ENCLOSURE
Consolidated farms of different sizes

The increase in agricultural productivity made the growth of cities possible. Overall, a smaller proportion of people could provide the food for the whole. England was the first large, modern state to make this leap. There were agricultural innovators in France who wanted to see a similar consolidation of holdings but the peasants there owned the land and were attached to their communal life; even an absolutist monarchy could not push them around.

From the mid-eighteenth century onward, the Industrial Revolution in England moved in lockstep with the Agricultural Revolution. Instead of cotton and wool being spun and woven by workers in their cottages, the business was transferred to factories, where new inventions, powered first by waterwheel and then by steam engines, did the work. The workers became custodians and maintainers of the equipment, working by the clock and for a boss instead of being their own master. The population of towns with cotton mills and woolen mills soared. All the new economic activity was knitted together first by a network of canals and then by the railways. There was at last a nation where bulk goods could be transported cheaply to every part of it.

England did not plan its Industrial Revolution. It was facilitated because in England, the parliament controlled the government. Absolutist governments in Europe planned, promoted, and protected industry in order to increase the economic and military power of the state. The nobility and landed gentlemen of England who composed the parliament were themselves involved in the new economic activity and were more inclined for it to be unfettered. The old rules regulating industry and employment were swept aside or allowed to expire.

The social changes produced by the two revolutions were traumatic. But the first urban, industrial nation held out the promise that the common people, who had lived so close to subsistence and had suffered so much, would be brought to an unimagined prosperity.

What Is It about Europe?

CHINESE CIVILIZATION WAS FOR A long period more advanced than European. From China, directly or indirectly, Europe acquired printing, papermaking, the compass, gunpowder, and locks for canals. Yet it was in Europe that steady economic growth first occurred and then the Industrial Revolution. And it was in Europe that representative government and individual rights, those other hallmarks of modernity, first developed. What is it about Europe?

In 1480, the Ming emperor of China ruled that overseas exploration and trade were forbidden; merchants who continued to trade were declared smugglers and troops were sent to destroy their settlements and burn their boats. No European king ever claimed or used such powers and no king could afford such a self-denying ordinance. In Europe, kings operated in a network of rival states; the Chinese emperor had the advantage—or the trap—of possessing no rivals of power equal to his own. The rivalry of states in Europe helped to impel them to overseas expansion.

After the fall of the Roman Empire in Western Europe, no single power has ever again controlled the whole territory. Imagine if a single power had conquered Rome as the Manchus did in China, the Mughals in India, and the Ottomans in the Middle East. By the act of conquest, they become masters of their new realm. The conquerors of Rome were various German tribes who were rivals of each other. They were masters of very little. They did not so much conquer the empire as discover that it was melting away beneath their feet. They had no experience of governing a settled state and could not maintain the Roman machinery of tax-gathering. They defied one of the universals of government by running states that were unable to tax.

Much of European history springs from this founding moment. Governments had the weakest hold on their people; they had to struggle and work hard to claim their allegiance. They had to offer good government—the king's peace—in return for extending their power. They could not simply run an apparatus for collecting tax and tribute as did so many empires and kingdoms in Asia and the Middle East.

For centuries, the threat to the king's control came from the mightiest of his subjects, the landed nobility. They were eventually subdued, but they had been strong enough on their own ground to gain for themselves and everyone else the security of private property. *Not everything is the king's*: This is the foundation of European liberty and its prosperity.

To subdue the nobility, the kings relied on the merchants, traders, and bankers of their towns, who provided loans and personnel for their bureaucracy and whose wealth could be taxed. European monarchs taxed in a regular, moderate way so that they did not kill the goose that laid the golden egg. Rulers of Asian states were more arbitrary, levying punitive taxes or simply confiscating the goods of merchants and traders if they were hard up. European monarchs were obliged to be prudent because they were one player in a finely balanced rivalry of states, and merchants pressed too hard could decamp to the rival states. They had to be interested in economic growth and in new technology, albeit chiefly the technology for war, but then as now defense spending had large spin-offs. Beyond prudence, they had the memory of the Roman Empire and the obligations cast upon a Christian prince to help keep them from tyranny and complete self-indulgence, which were much more commonly displayed in Asian kingdoms than in European.

As monarchs subdued the old nobility, they became patrons of a new, dynamic class: the urban bourgeoisie. When monarchs were still weak, they had allowed towns the right to govern themselves, which became a more significant concession as their wealth grew. Compared with nobles, who could command armed men and defend themselves in castles, the bourgeoisie seemed peaceful and unthreatening. But however fractious nobles were, they formed part of the social order of which kings were the natural heads; the bourgeoisie and their way of life had no need of kings and, in the long run, were much more disturbing to kingly rule than the nobility.

From their weak beginnings, monarchs gained in power, except in England, where monarchs were tamed by the parliament, an institution that survived from medieval times when kings were obliged to consult their great subjects. Even in France, the most renowned of the so-called absolute monarchies, the king did not command everywhere. To put his kingdom together he had needed to make many concessions and special deals. The Estates General of France no longer met but miniature Estates General survived in the outer provinces and played a part in rejecting the king's moves in the 1780s to reform the taxation system. And when his attempts failed, he was forced to revive the Estates General of France, a move imposed on him because the reformers were inspired by the English example of parliamentary government. In Central Europe, in what is now Germany and Italy, no monarch had established a strong state, a result of the emperor and the pope contesting for power. Here, there was a multitude of virtually independent states: cities, city-states, and princedoms, the extreme case of the dispersal of power in Europe. These ministates provided the base for the Renaissance and Reformation, which transformed the whole of Europe.

Though Europe was divided, it was one civilization, known in medieval times and beyond as Christendom. Until the Reformation, the church was the universal institution crossing all boundaries. It sometimes had ambitions to control the states, but though kings were obliged to be defenders of the faith, they did not see this as obliging them always to obey the commands of the church. The clash between emperor and pope was the most spectacular and long-lasting example of the constant tension between church and state, a further instance of the dispersal of power.

The common high culture of Christendom was controlled by the church. It was the guardian of its holy book, the Bible, and of the learning of Greece and Rome. In the Middle Ages, the scholars had woven both together to produce a coherent theology. The vulnerability of the church lay in its holy book being virtually silent on the church itself—an elaborate structure modeled on Roman rule—and in the learning it preserved from Rome, being the work of pagan authors. In the Reformation and Renaissance, the contradictions broke open.

In China, power was centered unequivocally in the emperor, and the high culture of Confucianism supported imperial rule. Confucianism was a guide to individual and public behavior and was embedded in society and the state. All who ruled officially and unofficially were well versed in it, and would-be bureaucrats had to pass examinations in it.

In Europe, power was dispersed and the high culture was composite and not firmly tethered to secular rule. The Chinese were very clever but their cleverness could never get out of control; the innovations were never fundamentally disruptive. The openness of European society goes a long way back. The dynamism of its economy and the turmoil of its intellectual life in the modern period derive from the fact that no single power was in charge, shaping it for good or ill. Its diverse inheritance could be fully explored and extended; the Greek faith in mathematics was realized during the Scientific Revolution, which in turn created a new basis for technological innovation.

Economic historians pose the question of why Europe was the first to industrialize, as if other societies were on the same trajectory and Europe reached the goal first. Patricia Crone, whose ideas have shaped so much of this book, asks the question: was Europe first or was it a freak? She has no doubt it was a freak.

Destructive Forces

EUROPE WAS *a group of* states and there was always conflict among them. In the twentieth century, European states fought two terrible wars in which soldiers and civilians were slaughtered on a new mass scale. During the second war, Nazi Germany under Adolf Hitler tried systematically to exterminate European Jews, a horror without parallel in European history. How had this happened?

Two forces to which you have already been introduced played a large part: nationalism, which had its intellectual origins in Germany, and industrialization, which began in Britain.

Nationalism strengthened the attachment of people to their state and their willingness to fight and die for it. Nationalism made people struggle to create their own state if they did not have one. This was a great source of conflict in the countries of central and Eastern Europe, which now become players in our history.

Industrialization attracted people away from the countryside and into the more anonymous society of the towns. Populations grew rapidly; people were massed together as they had not been before. They learned to read. They learned about their society in school and from newspapers, which were mass-produced cheaply on machinery run by steam. In the twentieth century, they were listening to the radio and watching films. Hitler was a radio person and a new kind of film star. As old social ties weakened and the church became less important, national feeling, inculcated in schools and spread by new media, helped knit people together. Nationalism acted as a substitute for religion, giving individuals a place in an everlasting community. Not Christians in Christendom, but French in France, or Germans in Germany. There were anthems and flags, heroes and heroines, and sacred moments and places, to secure attachment to this new faith.

If nationalism made for war, industrialization made war more terrible. The new iron and steel mills could produce larger and more destructive weapons and in greater number. Guns had once been handmade, with the craftsman ensuring that all the moving parts fit together. But with the development of accurate machine tools all the parts could be made exactly the same, which allowed for rapid, mass production. In fact, guns were the first products to be made in this way, sixty years before cars were.

In Europe, there was a new scale in human affairs: mass production; mass society; mass slaughter.

Industrialization produced a new internal threat to the societies of Europe. Peasants had regularly revolted and had fairly easily been suppressed. Workers in the new industrial towns worked and lived more closely together; as they learned to read and write they came to understand the forces that controlled them and created organizations that had a permanent existence. Through these, they made their claims for a better life and a say in the running of their society.

Workers formed protest movements to demand political rights, chief among them the right of all men to vote. They organized trade unions to fight their bosses for better wages and conditions. They formed political parties with the aim of removing bosses and profit and having industry run for the good of those who did the work: This was the program of socialism. Or despairing of any real change by peaceful means, they planned revolution to get rid of bosses and establish a workers' state. These communist revolutionaries had no lasting success in Europe; they did succeed in Russia, and the fear their rule in Russia provoked was a potent force in Europe. Nationalists hated communists because communists claimed that workers should not fight for their countries; workers of all the lands, they said, should cooperate and fight only their bosses and the governments that protected those bosses.

Industrialization also swelled the ranks of the middle class, and the merchants, bankers, manufacturers, and professional people who served them. They were an old class; they became important once trade and industry had started to grow. Absolute monarchs had drawn on their wealth and had recruited them into their service. In the nineteenth and twentieth centuries, growing in numbers and confidence, they were the group most committed to liberal policies, that is, to representative government, to the rule of law, and to individual rights and liberties—freedom of the press and association and freedom for businesses to make money. All these policies were directed against rule by kings and aristocrats. On the other hand, liberals did not want power to pass to the people; they were not democrats. To what extent would they support or oppose popular demands? This was a constant dilemma. Workers faced the same problem; could they accept the leadership of middle-class liberals in battles against privilege or would the workers be used and betrayed?

How these forces played out in the three leading countries of Europe in the nineteenth century is what we will examine first. Did industrialization lead to revolution?

CHAPTER 9

Industrialization and Revolution

THE INDUSTRIAL revolution in Britain was unplanned and there was no planning in the cities that grew around the new factories. To accommodate the workers, old houses were rented out by the room, from attic to cellar; one room was the living space for a whole family. New row houses were built, crammed together, back to back, so you had a front door but no back door or back windows either. The roads were unpaved; there were no sewers or gutters; filth of every kind accumulated in the streets and on waste ground.

In the 1840s, a young man from Germany inspected all this and wrote a passionate book of denunciation and prophecy, *The Condition of the Working Class in England*. The author was Friedrich Engels, who came to England to do a stint in his father's business that manufactured sewing threads. He was in a theoretical way a communist; in England he discovered, he thought, the forces that would bring his ideals to reality. He wrote that no people had ever lived the way the English now lived. Making goods by machinery had polarized society: There

Old houses in Manchester into which workers and their families crowded.

were in the new towns only two classes: the middle-class owners of the factories and the workers. The work itself was monotonous and demeaning; the workers had nothing but their work to live on, so a downturn in trade left them destitute—good workers as much as the bad; they were housed as if to test "in how little space a human being can move, how little air . . . he can breathe, how little of civilization he may share and yet live." Engels concluded that this situation could not last. It was a scientific certainty that there would be an eruption, a workers' revolt that would make the French Revolution look like child's play.

Engels published his book in German. Its most important reader was Karl Marx, a German philosopher turned revolutionary journalist. Marx and Engels teamed up and in 1848 published *The Communist Manifesto*, which declared that all history was moving toward the situation that Engels had described in England. Just as the middle class had struggled against the aristocracy, so the workers would overthrow the middle class and establish a communist workers' state. "The history of all hitherto existing society," said the opening words of *The Communist Manifesto*, "is the history of class struggle." Its concluding advice to workers was that in overturning society they would lose nothing but their chains; law and religion in existing societies operated only to oppress them. Individual rights—what we now call human rights—were a fraud too; they benefited the bosses and did nothing for the workers.

Their little book was the most influential political pamphlet published in the nineteenth and twentieth centuries—but not because its predictions were correct. According to the theory, the workers' revolution would happen first where capitalism was most advanced—this meant England. In England, there was political change, but no workers' revolution.

England's revolution of the seventeenth century had produced a constitution in which the monarch was controlled by parliament. There was no uniform system for the election of the parliament.

Different rules applied in different places as to who could vote in elections. Overall, only one man in six had the vote, and working men were excluded. Towns whose population had shrunk or even disappeared continued to elect one or two members of parliament. So who did the electing when the town ceased to exist? The man who owned the ground on which the town had stood. Meanwhile, many of the new towns of the industrial revolution had no members at all.

Moves to reform parliament had begun in the late eighteenth century. These came to a halt with the French Revolution, which showed how reform could get out of hand. Reformers themselves did not want to stir the pot, and any working-class movements in England that took up the French notion of the rights of man were suppressed. In the 1820s, the push for reform recommenced. Reform for the middle class meant chiefly ending the hold that the aristocracy and the landed gentry had over the parliament. This would be achieved by giving more representation to the towns, the real towns, and perhaps voting by secret ballot so the great land-owners could no longer tell their tenants how they must vote. For working men, reform meant, first of all, votes for all men.

The opposition party in parliament took up the cause of reform. This was the Whig Party, who were not themselves middle-class men; far from it, they were more aristocratic than the governing Tory Party. The Whigs were the party who had carried through the seventeenth-century revolution against the Catholic king James II. They saw themselves as the guardians of the rights that all Englishmen enjoyed and of the English way of constitutional monarchy. After a long period in opposition, they came to power in 1830, and in 1832, after a huge struggle, carried the first measure of parliamentary reform. It was fiercely resisted by the Tory Party and the House of Lords, where the Tories had a majority. It was carried because working men rallied in support in huge demonstrations and processions, which made it look as if violence or revolution would follow if the reform were rejected.

The Reform Act of 1832 gave the vote to the middle class and wiped out the representation of the tiny or nonexistent towns. Workers had given their support even though the reform did not give them the vote. They were exhilarated by this attack on the old order and felt that more change would soon follow.

When more change did not occur, leaders of the working class developed their own program for a completely democratic state. It was proclaimed in the People's Charter of 1838, and its supporters were known as the Chartists. The six points it contained were: votes for all men, equal electorates, secret ballot, no property qualifications for members of parliament, payment of members, and annual parliaments.

The Chartists' method was to elect delegates to a national convention, draw up petitions to parliament asking for the adoption of the Charter, and have them signed by millions. But what if parliament rejected their petition? The Chartists were divided: Most wanted to continue with "moral force"; some to turn to "physical force." The debate was ongoing because on three occasions over ten years parliament rejected the petition. Engels was right to this extent: The most determined Chartists were in the new factory towns of the north. They tried and failed to run a general strike when the second petition was rejected. The plan was to stay on strike until the Charter was granted.

The Chartist petition of 1842, signed by more than three million people, being carried to parliament.

A lot of the talk about violence was bluff; the Chartists wanted to scare the government into agreeing with them. But the government was not scared; the middle class, now part of the political nation, stood with the aristocracy and the gentry against yielding anything to the Chartists. It is when ruling classes are disunited that revolutionaries have their chance. The Chartists knew there was little hope of force prevailing, which is why the moral approach kept winning in their ranks. After each rebuff they returned to petitioning.

The government did not ban the chartist movement. It sought to control it rather than suppress it. The government and the courts declared that public meetings were quite lawful; asking for all men to have the vote was lawful; petitioning was more than lawful—it was an ancient right. What was unlawful were meetings that ended in rioting, and seditious talk at meetings and in newspapers that brought the government into contempt or threatened violence. It was for these offenses that Chartists were arrested, and tried in open court with the usual standards of evidence. They were mostly found guilty, but the punishment, six or twelve months in prison, was light.

The government was determined not to have to kill Chartists, which would outrage public opinion and enrage their followers. This shows how genuinely liberal a society England had become. Elsewhere, nothing would better please aristocrats and the middle class than a slaughter of their working-class enemies. The government sent troops to control the Chartists, but the general in charge sympathized with them and used his troops with great discretion.

Even when the Chartists were petitioning, their leaders did not think that political rights were all they needed. Some worked on educating the workers; others on keeping them off the drink; others on settling them on small landholdings; others on trade unions; others on creating socialist cooperatives. By these means, working people were becoming respectable members of civil society. These activities continued when the Chartist movement died out after 1850.

The three great Chartist agitations in the 1830s and 1840s had coincided with economic depression; after 1850, there were good years and the standard of living for workers improved. Then in 1866, with very little outside pressure, a government of the Liberal Party (the successor to the Whigs) proposed to widen the franchise. The Tory Party boldly outbid the Liberals and in 1867 carried a measure that gave the vote to most of the workers in the towns. In 1884, a Liberal government gave the vote to country workers. The second and third Reform Acts still did not establish manhood suffrage; an elector had to be a householder or a lodger. Many soldiers fighting for Britain in World War I were not eligible to vote. By the end of the war, they were eligible because in 1918 the fourth Reform Act established virtual manhood suffrage and gave some women, only those over thirty, the vote.

So the rulers of Britain managed the social disruption of the industrial revolution without political disruption. In stages, the ancient constitution was widened to include the workingman, and Britain gained its reputation as the most stable of countries.

IN FRANCE, THERE WAS NO industrial revolution. The making of textiles became mechanized but the coal and iron industries did not expand rapidly. Throughout the nineteenth century, France was an agricultural society, with much of the land in the hands of peasants, who were owners of their lands because of the 1789 revolution.

In the ten years after 1789, France instituted various forms of government. After absolute monarchy, there came constitutional monarchy, a democratic republic, a property owners' republic, and military dictatorship. Then France tried them all again in slower motion through the nineteenth century. The instability was permanent because the divisions created during the course of the first revolution took a long time to heal. No form of government could command general assent. Everyone had seen what their enemies were capable of. Even the moderate revolutionaries of 1789–91 had attacked the Catholic church, so the church and the faithful thought they were safe only with a restored monarchy or, as second best, a strongman like Napoleon. The liberals could give no quarter to the Catholic church because that spelled reaction and loss of liberty. Workers could be useful allies to liberals but they were scared of what workers might do: The more democratic the revolution of 1789 had become, the more tyrannical.

Regime change was a constant option and failed revolutions and coups regular events. Because even liberal regimes were under threat, they closed down newspapers and banned organizations—and so encouraged another revolution. Among the failed revolutions were attempts to establish workers' states—in a country where there was limited industrial development and only a small working class.

Here is a chart of France's political history.

1815	1830	1848	1870
RESTORATION	REVOLUTION	REVOLUTION	DEFEAT IN WAR
Bourbon Monarchs	*Orleanist Monarch*	*Democratic Republic*	*Democratic Republic*
Louis XVIII	*Louis Philippe*	*1848–51*	*1870–1940*
Charles X			
		Failed Socialist Revolution	*Paris Commune eliminated 1871*
		Napoleon III Emperor 1851–70	*Failed attempt at monarchy*
			Republic secure 1879

After Napoleon I was defeated in 1815, the European allies that had been battling him restored the House of Bourbon to the throne. So there was another King Louis, the eighteenth. He was not to be an absolute ruler, but the people had no *right* to a say in government. Louis allowed that there could be a parliament, which had very few powers, and for which very few people had the

Revolutionary tradition: Delacroix depicts the 1830 revolution in *Liberty Leading the People*.

right to vote. His brother, Charles, a true reactionary, succeeded him, and was swept away in the revolution of 1830.

The next monarch was to be a constitutional monarch: Louis Philippe, the citizen king. He came from the house of Orléans, which was related to the Bourbons but progressive. His father had supported the revolution of 1789 and had gone under the name Philippe Égalité. Louis Philippe was not committed to equality; more people could vote for his parliaments but still not the workers. The revolution that removed him in 1848 established a democratic republic. The constitution it drew up included an elected president. The first presidential election was won by Louis Napoleon, nephew of the first Napoleon. His period of office was four years with no renewal; before it was over, he seized power in a coup and ruled as emperor, aiming at the glory of his uncle and notably failing. In 1870, he was captured by the Prussians, with whom foolishly he had gone to war. A democratic republic replaced him.

The republic had a rocky start. Its first elections returned an anti-republic majority, so for a time, the parliament was trying to reestablish a monarchy, for which there were rival candidates from the Houses of Bourbon and Orléans. The people of Paris, not wanting to be ruled by an anti-republican regime, created briefly their own government, the Commune, which was suppressed by the republic. The national republican vote rose so that by 1879 the republic was reasonably secure.

The Paris Commune was the last and most determined effort of the people of Paris to make a revolution their own. From 1789, they provided the street fighters for all the revolutions. Not for them a debate over whether physical force was legitimate. If there was half an opening, they would raid the gun shops for weapons, proclaim a republic, sing the *Marseillaise,* throw up barricades across the streets, and prepare to do battle. But the new regime was always a disappointment. In 1832, the people rose up against Louis Philippe, whom they had assisted to power two years before. The uprising was crushed with the loss of hundreds of lives. In 1848, workingmen and their representatives were part of the first revolutionary government. To please them, daily working hours were reduced to ten in Paris and eleven in the provinces, and national workshops were established, not run for profit, to provide work for the unemployed. But after the first elections the republic turned more conservative and the national workshops were closed. The people staged a revolt, which was put down with perhaps 3,000 being killed.

In the Commune for ten weeks the people were in charge. They were republican, anti-priest, and socialist. Their attacks on the church and the clergy were ferocious; they used churches for storing weapons and for political meetings and executed one of their hostages, the Archbishop of Paris. They encouraged the formation of cooperative workshops and declared that outstanding bills and rent did not have to be paid. Bakers were freed from having to work through the night so socialism meant no fresh rolls for breakfast—in Paris!

The people who led and supported the Commune were not factory workers—Paris was not an industrial city; they were laborers, building workers, and skilled workers from small workshops, together with students, journalists, and the regular revolutionaries. Socialism had become a part of the workers' agenda, not because working conditions had changed, but because Paris, the heartland of revolution, was the natural home for new ideas of working-class liberation.

But France was never going to support the aims of the Parisian workers. They made the revolutions but when elections were held, the peasants, the great mass of the population, could be very readily persuaded to vote to save private property or the church. In 1871, the Communards recognized this and declared that each area of France should rule itself just as they were ruling Paris; they were not imposing themselves on the whole country. The new republican government, sitting for the moment at Versailles with its monarchical majority, was never going to accept that. It sent the troops to retake Paris for France. Twenty thousand Communards were killed in the street fighting and the summary executions that followed. This was not simply a military operation; it was an act of class hatred and political cleansing.

Socialists and communists took great hope from the fact that briefly there had been a workers' government. Marx welcomed the breaking out of class war in France, though the reasons for it were not quite as he and Engels had predicted. He thought the Communards had not been ruthless enough. They should have marched out to Versailles and toppled the new republican government before it established itself and imposed its rule on France. The need to be ruthless, not to seek support but seize power, was also the lesson drawn by Lenin, who was to be the leader of the communist revolution in Russia.

The brutal suppression of the Commune stopped the working-class threat to French society. Once the republic was secure, workers' associations in trade unions and socialist parties were allowed. Some workers were still attached to revolution, but a stable republic was not going to offer them the breakdown in authority that had previously given workers their chance. Nevertheless, it was a democratic republic: The workers did have and keep the vote. The republic lasted until the fall of France in 1940.

GERMANY HAD ITS INDUSTRIAL revolution late, in the second half of the nineteenth century. It was a third-stage industrial revolution, with chemical and electrical industries being prominent, as well as textiles (first stage) and coal and iron (second stage). German industrial workers supported the largest socialist party in Europe, which for a long time kept to the teachings of Marx. This made them opposed to war in a society that possessed the most efficient war machine in Europe.

Germany did not become united until 1871, just as its industrial revolution was taking off. Previously, the various German states were linked in a very loose confederation, which had been set up by the Allied nations who had beaten Napoleon in 1815. This confederation replaced the Holy Roman Empire that Napoleon had abolished. Germany provided the deep thinkers about nationalism, its roots and its necessity, in part because when they wrote there was no German nation.

Much stood in the way of Germany's becoming a nation. The individual states valued their independence and enjoyed the attachment of their people, even though nationalism was a growing force. The two largest German states, Prussia and Austria, were rivals, with neither wanting the other to organize a German nation and become the dominant player within it. A united Germany would be a new power in Europe, which made the other powers very watchful of any moves to create a German union.

In 1848, suddenly a new way to union opened up. The revolution in Paris in that year sparked revolutions across Europe, including Germany. But not in England: The Chartists collected another petition, but when the police told a mass rally that it could not go in strength to parliament to present it, the crowd dispersed. In Europe, the crowds pushed on and frightened rulers into granting liberal and democratic concessions, most of which they were able to withdraw after the revolutionary moment passed and liberals became frightened of democrats. But while all was in flux, elected representatives from the German states gathered in Frankfurt to found a German nation.

They were an assembly of great substance and talent: professors, judges, administrators, professional men, some few businessmen, mostly liberal in their politics, with a democratic minority. They had to decide first where the boundaries of the new nation were to be drawn; if all of Austria were included that would encompass many non-Germans. They decided to exclude Austria. They issued a declaration of basic rights and drew up a constitution that gave all men the vote in the lower house of parliament. Should an elected president or an elected monarch be at its head, or should an existing monarch be the leader? They decided to offer the role to the king of Prussia—and he declined. He had no wish to be a ruler under a liberal constitution and he knew that this assembly did not really have the power it claimed: What would Austria think? What would other powers think if he stood forward as ruler of Germany?

The assembly began its work when there was a power vacuum. When it reached its conclusion, the monarchs and princes were back in control and able to ignore the assembly. Some of the democrats in the assembly wanted to push on with revolution, to remove the old rulers and establish the new nation, but the liberals would have none of that, for they were afraid of where revolution would lead. The liberals' failure at Frankfurt damaged them as makers of the nation.

The nation would not be made by speeches and majority votes; it would be made by blood and iron: These were the sentiments of Otto von Bismarck, chief minister under the king of Prussia from 1862, a master of diplomacy and of war. In 1866, he contrived a war with Austria, which Prussia rapidly won. In the peace settlement, the north German states that had supported Prussia and those that had made the mistake of supporting Austria were brought into a North German Federation under Prussian control. Then he contrived for France to declare war on Prussia. This was a landmark in European diplomacy and war: Bismarck got France to do what he wanted by doctoring a press release, more particularly a telegram from his king, that reported that a dispute with France over who should take the throne of Spain had been settled.

Bismarck edited the telegram so that it read as if the king had rebuffed France over the issue, and then he released it to the press. There was outrage in France at this insult; the national honor was at stake; Napoleon III declared war.

Bismarck wanted war at this time because he reckoned correctly that the other powers would not intervene and that under cover of war he could get the southern German states to

The iron chancellor: Otto von Bismarck.

join his federation. France was nominally the protector of their independence so as to prevent the emergence of too great a Germany. But now France was the aggressor, and very soon the Prussian army had encircled the French armies and their hapless emperor, and for the moment, France was powerless. The southern states came on board. The king of the southern state of Bavaria, speaking for the rulers of all the German states, proposed that the king of Prussia become German emperor (in a script provided by Bismarck!). William I was proclaimed emperor in the palace at Versailles.

The German Empire was in essence a Prussian Empire. King William of Prussia and his chief minister, Bismarck, were also German emperor and German chancellor. The German army and the civil service were composed largely of Prussians and run on Prussian lines. The Prussian capital, Berlin, became the German capital. Bismarck did provide a parliament, the Reichstag, for the new nation. It had no control over the chancellor and his policies; it was the body that passed laws and approved the annual budget. The military budget had to be approved only every seven years. If the Reichstag questioned military spending, Bismarck contrived a national crisis to bring it into line.

Prussia began as a small state on the eastern frontier of German lands in what is now Poland. Its landowning aristocracy, the Junkers, gave the character to the state; they were resolute in protecting their order and fierce opponents of liberalism and democracy; they officered the army and took the military life with its discipline, service, and high sense of honor as the ideal. The efficiency of Prussia's army had carried this small marginal state to greatness. Now Prussia gave its character to the new German state. The liberals, who had wanted a nation created and controlled by the citizens, mostly accepted the union that Bismarck had delivered. Bismarck was himself a Junker, though the Junkers could not understand or appreciate that their order was being protected by someone as flexible and opportunistic as Bismarck.

Bismarck was opposed to democracy but he provided that all men would have a vote for the Reichstag. The emperor was appalled when Bismarck first revealed his support for universal suffrage. "This is revolution," he said. Bismarck replied: "What can that matter to Your Majesty, if universal suffrage puts you on a rock where the waters can never reach you?" So a democratic Reichstag was to keep liberals and democrats quiet; the trick was then to manage it so that emperor and chancellor could still rule as they wished. The Reichstag could not remove Bismarck, but he had to find support there to pass his measures. He found it where he could: He used liberals when he wanted to get rid of trade restrictions within the empire and limit the power of the Catholic church (Prussia was largely Protestant; the newly acquired southern states Catholic); he used conservatives when he decided that agriculture needed to be protected and socialists controlled. He would not accept that he could be thwarted by the Reichstag, still less that he should gradually allow it to become like the British parliament, the body that controlled governments. The liberals in the Reichstag theoretically wanted that, but they were too respectful of authority and too afraid of democracy to bring on a struggle to get it.

The party of the socialists, the Social Democratic Party, grew in strength in the Reichstag. It was the one party that would never give support to Bismarck. He, in turn, hated the socialists. He was horrified by the Paris Commune, which took over the city when the Prussian army was in France, and he hated it more after the leader of the Social Democrats openly praised the Commune in the Reichstag. After an attempt was made to assassinate the emperor in 1878, Bismarck passed laws that banned socialist organizing and publications. However, socialists were still allowed to be elected to the Reichstag. So Germany took the opposite path from Britain in meeting a working-class challenge. Britain allowed Chartists to organize but not vote; Germany allowed socialists to vote but not organize. The effect was to alienate socialist supporters from German society; socialist organizing continued but now it was underground.

Bismarck then tried to lure workers away from socialism by making himself a pioneer in the provision of social welfare by the state: He introduced old-age pensions and accident and health insurance. This did not work either. The socialist vote continued to rise.

In 1888, Germany acquired a new emperor, William II, the grandson of William I. He was bright, active, and ambitious for his country, but impulsive, almost juvenile in his wants and moods, in no way prudent or measured, and very confident that he could rule without needing the assistance of the old man Bismarck. He and Bismarck disagreed about socialism. Bismarck wanted to make permanent his anti-socialist legislation; the emperor was, of course, opposed to socialism but thought he could limit its appeal by gentler methods. So Bismarck resigned. The anti-socialist laws were lifted and new laws passed to regulate hours and conditions of work.

The Social Democratic Party flourished, becoming in the early twentieth century the largest of the parties, with one in three Germans voting for it. Politically, that still gave it little influence since policy was determined by the emperor and his chancellor. Social Democrats did not become ministers, nor did their party want them to join any government that was not socialist. Socially, the party encouraged its supporters to live apart in cultural and sporting associations that the party ran. Partly this was to protect workers from the corruption of middle-class society, partly because the middle class was not in any case disposed to mix with workers. So this great new force in German life remained isolated and corralled.

The party was divided over policy. Marx had been a great inspiration for it but now "revisionists" argued that Marx's predictions were not coming true: Workers were not becoming poorer, the standard of living was rising; society was not being reduced to just two classes, workers and bosses, for there was a growing group of white-collar workers; the state was improving workers' conditions. This meant that the party should work for socialism through existing channels and not look to crisis and breakdown and revolution. Most Social Democrats in the Reichstag, in practice, accepted this view, but revisionism was officially rejected by the party. To please the party faithful you had to speak of revolution. This meant that social democracy remained an object of dread to the rest of German society.

Here in summary is how industrialization and revolution worked out in Britain, France, and Germany by the beginning of the twentieth century:

BRITAIN	FRANCE	GERMANY
• *history of monarchs controlled by parliament*	• *history of revolution*	• *history of autocratic government*
• *industrial revolution*	• *limited industrialization*	• *rapid industrialization*
• *middle class enfranchised*	• *failed workers' revolutions*	• *large socialist party preaching revolution*
• *workers' democratic demands rejected— and later accepted*	• *democratic but not socialist republic*	• *autocracy corrals Social Democrats*

The political affairs of Britain and France had reached some sort of stability. In Germany, it was not yet resolved how the new class of workers was to be accommodated in the state.

MARX HAD CALLED ON THE workers of all lands to unite. Marx himself helped form an international organization of workers in 1864. This fell apart in arguments between socialists and anarchists. A second international was formed in 1889. Delegates from the countries of Europe and a few from outside Europe met regularly in congresses. They debated how socialists should respond to war so that workers would not be slaughtered for the benefit of their bosses. The options were: socialists in parliament refusing to vote finance for war, a general strike, and sabotaging the war effort. Lenin, the communist leader from Russia, had a different approach. In Russia, still backward economically, there was very little industrialization so he could not rely on mass support of workers to stop war. Instead, he said the demands of war would weaken governments and that would give a determined group of workers the opportunity to stage a revolution and destroy capitalism.

Russia was governed by autocratic rulers, the tsars. In 1905, Tsar Nicholas II had been forced to allow a parliament, the Duma, to operate but it did not control the government. Tsar Nicholas and his ministers were desperate to catch up with Western Europe so the limited industrialization in Russia had been encouraged by the government. The new heavy industries were concentrated in the large cities of St. Petersburg and Moscow. Having heavy industry and industrial workers concentrated in the capital was not the usual pattern of industrialization in Western Europe. It made the tsar more vulnerable.

When the great powers went to war in August 1914, Russia fought with France and Britain against Germany and Austria. It was the first country to crumple under the stress of World War I, which made huge demands on men and materials. Early in 1917, there were strikes in the factories of St. Petersburg and Moscow and mutinies of soldiers. Workers and soldiers formed councils— or soviets—to take power into their own hands. The tsar abdicated and a provisional government was formed, which planned to hold elections for a constituent assembly to draw up a constitution. This government planned to carry on the war, but since reform had been promised, the mutinies and desertions grew apace. The peasants threw away their arms and set off for home.

The communists now had their chance. Lenin ran a small, tightly knit organization that was ready to seize power and take Russia out of the war. His section of the communist movement was called the Bolsheviks (majority); the Mensheviks (minority) wanted to work with other reformers and not rush to revolution. The Bolsheviks gained control of the workers' and soldiers' soviets and in November 1917, Lenin organized an almost bloodless revolution to topple the provisional government. The blood came after the revolution. The Bolsheviks closed down the constituent assembly, assumed dictatorial powers for themselves, seized businesses and property without compensation, attacked the church and killed priests, and enforced their rule with a secret police that tortured and murdered. But Lenin did have a popular

Lenin addresses soldiers and workers.

slogan—peace, bread, land—that meant an end to war, more to eat, and the farm you wanted. The peasants for the moment were to be given their land—even though communists were opposed to individual ownership. Communism was to be attempted in Russia even though Marx taught that communist revolution would happen first in advanced capitalist countries and that backward ones were in no sense ready for it. Lenin had been right: The strain of war, which was not part of Marx's theory, would provide the revolutionary opportunity.

The Russian revolution was a momentous event in world history because there was now a large state ruled by communists in the name of the workers. Marx had presented what he saw as the science by which industrial societies would be overthrown by a workers' revolution. His "scientific" predictions were wrong; what his "science" did was to encourage communists to think that revolution was inevitable, that history was on their side, and that they had the right to rule ruthlessly—which led to success in places most unlikely according to Marxist theory. Russia was a surprise in 1917; China in 1949 was bizarre.

Lenin knew that communism could not be easily built in a backward country of peasants; he hoped that the revolution in Russia would be the spur to revolutions throughout Europe, which would destroy capitalism and allow workers everywhere to establish communism. Radical workers everywhere did take heart from the establishment of a workers' state and hoped to imitate it. In Germany, they had some short-lived success. This too was because of World War I, more precisely because of Germany's defeat in it.

We will now examine the origins of this war, which gave communists their chance—and brought a terrible reaction.

CHAPTER 10

Two World Wars

ONCE BISMARCK had created Germany, his adventurism in war was over; he wanted to preserve the peace in Europe. There were five great powers in Europe and his aim was always to be in an alliance of three.

The states of Europe after the unification of Germany are shown on the map.

The new German Empire was much bigger than Germany is today. After losses in two world wars, Germany's possessions in the east have been much reduced. Poland now stands on what were Prussia's eastern territories.

Italy, like Germany, had only recently been united and its moves to union followed the same pattern as Germany's. With the collapse

The states of Europe after the unification of Germany.

of authority in the 1848 revolutions, a democratic republic for all Italy had been proclaimed in Rome. That was suppressed. Then Cavour, the chief minister of the northern state of Piedmont, united Italy by smart diplomacy and force. His king, Victor Emmanuel II, became the king of Italy in 1861. The last state to be acquired by the new nation was the pope's, whose territory was still a substantial band across the center of the peninsula. After the upheavals of 1848, Napoleon III of France had sent an army to protect the pope. When Napoleon lost to Prussia in 1870, Italy was able to take over Rome.

To the east of the new nations of Germany and Italy were the sprawling empires of Russia and Austria, economically backward compared to Western Europe. These were multiethnic societies containing peoples who now saw themselves as subjected nations. The Magyars of Hungary had made themselves such a threat to Austria that it agreed in 1867 to share power with them in a joint monarchy under the name Austro-Hungarian Empire.

There was a third multiethnic empire in Europe, that of the Ottoman Turks, who ruled from Istanbul (formerly Constantinople). This empire was in decline, which gave the peoples of the Balkans the chance to make their own nations. It was a perilous course. Having conceded their right to a separate existence, Turkey still wanted to keep some control over them. Austria and Russia welcomed the breakup of the Turkish Empire but they did not want the new nations to be too independent either, for they had their own interests in this part of the world. Russia wanted to replace Turkey in Europe so it would have uninterrupted access from the Black Sea through the straits at Istanbul into the Mediterranean. Austria, having lost out to Prussia in Northern Europe, did not want to lose out to Russia in the southeast. So this was the battleground of Europe; there would always be conflict. Turkey continued to decline, which gave nationalists hope; the new nations formed out of Turkey were an encouragement to those still under Austrian or Russian control; the forces of national liberation clashed with the strategic interests of the great powers. Furthermore, the new nations and nations-to-be had claims against each other, since the peoples were mixed and territory had more than one claimant.

The five great powers were Britain, France, Germany, Austria, and Russia. Italy wanted to be the sixth but, though a player in the system of alliances, it did not carry much weight. For Bismarck, Germany's best allies were Russia and Austria, ruled by emperors, like Germany. The republic of France, after its defeat by Prussia in 1870, was never going to be a German ally. It nursed deep feelings of revenge because, after the war, Germany had seized its eastern provinces of Alsace and Lorraine. They were largely German-speaking and the German generals wanted the advantage of having German territory across the Rhine. Britain tended to be isolationist regarding Europe; its interests lay overseas, though its settled policy was not to allow one power to dominate the continent.

Russia and Austria gave Bismarck his group of three but it was very difficult to hold on to both allies because they were at odds in the Balkans. Like it or not, Bismarck had to get involved in Balkan affairs and keep both empires onside. If Germany backed Austria too strongly in Balkan disputes, Russia might look to France as an ally. Then Bismarck's nightmare would be realized: If war came, Germany would be fighting on two fronts. There was no one better than Bismarck at this juggling, and until his departure, he kept his alliance of three alive—just.

William II and his chancellors gave up on keeping both Russia and Austria as allies. They committed Germany wholeheartedly to Austria with the inevitable result: In 1893, Russia struck an alliance with France. Then in 1904, Britain reached an entente (an agreement) with France. The details of this pact related to the settlement of their disputes over the territories they were claiming outside Europe; there was no commitment to aiding France in a European war, but since France was the ancient enemy, this new alliance was highly significant. Germany and Austria were now two in a group of five. Bringing Italy onside did not help much (and during World War I, it changed sides).

Confident of Germany's power, William II and his ministers were not distressed at the loss of Russia as an ally. The Austrians as German-speakers were more congenial than the backward and, as they saw them, barbaric Slavs of the east—something that would not have weighed with Bismarck, who went to war with Austria to secure a German union under Prussian control. But now Germany did have to prepare for a war on two fronts. The plan entailed a quick knockout blow against France, then the turning of Germany's full might on Russia.

Prussia and then Germany had mastered the logistics of mobilizing and moving forces quickly; they used trains to transport troops and the telegraph to monitor and direct them. In 1870, Prussia had defeated France in the short space of six months; the plan for the next war had this done in six weeks. The other powers followed Germany's example and drew up plans for rapid mobilization; they were primed for war.

Not content with being the great land power in Europe, Germany proceeded to build a substantial navy. This was a pet project of the emperor's, who could not stand Britain's preeminence in this field. Britain's command of the seas was essential for the survival of its empire and for its own survival, since it did not grow enough food to feed itself. It was alarmed by Germany's shipbuilding and set out to show it could outmatch it. A naval arms race set in, with the people in both countries cheering and panicking in turn. Newspapers and politicians drummed up this nationalist feeling, which was a new element in defense planning. Winston Churchill, minister in the British government, said that at one point the navy demanded six new battleships; the economists said only four could be afforded—"we finally compromised on eight."

That war would break out was widely assumed. There seemed almost a welcoming of war. New strands of thought about racial strength and the survival of the fittest made war seem a proper test of nationhood. You could only think that if the war was going to be short and swift—which was what nearly everyone did think.

Germany was the disturbing element among the great powers. It was bound to seek greater influence as its economic power grew, but in July 1914, its military leaders risked all on a victory in a general European war. The opportunity they seized was a crisis in the Balkans. When Archduke Franz Ferdinand, the heir to the throne of Austria-Hungary, was visiting Bosnia in the far south of the empire, he was assassinated by a Serbian nationalist. Bosnia was home to many Serbs who were encouraged by elements in Serbia to rebel against Austria. Serbia itself was at first helped to its independence from Turkey by Austria; now Austria saw Serbia as a subversive force. As it was threatened by Austria, Serbia looked to Russia for protection.

The Austrian government knew if it were too tough on Serbia, which it held responsible for the assassination, it might provoke war with Russia. Germany encouraged it to be tough and the emperor himself pledged his backing for whatever Austria did. Austria thus made demands on Serbia designed to be so harsh that Serbia must resist them and, in doing so, give Austria the grounds for war. Now the other powers saw the danger if Serbia resisted and was backed by Russia. They, including Russia itself, looked for ways to avoid war. Germany pretended to the other powers that it had nothing to do with Austria's harsh demands on Serbia and frustrated all attempts at a peaceful settlement. Germany's military leaders wanted Russia to be provoked into war by Austria. They wanted to fight Russia now before its program to improve its military capacity was complete. If Russia became too strong, then it would be impossible to win the war on two fronts. The emperor did not want this wider war, but he was sidelined by the chancellor and the military.

Moltke, the head of the German army, was in a hurry to get the war started; he would need to defeat France quickly before Russia could get organized. But it was important for Russia to mobilize first so that it, rather than Germany, would appear as the aggressor. The Social Democratic Party was opposed to war; it had condemned Austria's harsh approach to Serbia, but it would support a defensive war if Russia was the aggressor. Russia did mobilize to deter Austria, which delighted the German military, for now Germany could declare war on Russia. Germany proclaimed Russia as the aggressor in the war that had been engineered in Berlin. France mobilized to defend itself against Germany.

The plan to conquer France in six weeks was put into action. It required the German armies to pass through Belgium and enter France from the north. They were to swing south in a huge arc enveloping Paris and then move east and take the French armies in the rear as they were attacking across the Franco-German border. The Germans asked Belgium for permission for their armies' passage and were refused. They marched their armies in regardless and, in doing so, violated Belgium's neutrality of which they were one of the guarantors. There was outrage in Britain at this German ruthlessness. It was not certain that Britain would have joined the war; the violation of Belgium determined it.

In a speech to the Reichstag, William II went for the big lie and declared Germany had done everything to avoid war. The members from the Social Democratic Party may not have believed him, but they voted with the rest to pass unanimously the first installment of war-finance. They did believe they would be worse off if Russia won. In every country where socialists had seats in parliament, they voted to support war. Nationalism had triumphed. The workers were to fight each other after all.

THE GERMAN PLAN for the invasion of France failed. The great sweep of armed might was not quite strong enough; the armies passed to the north of Paris rather than enveloping it and French and British forces were able to attack their flank. Soon there was stalemate; the opposing forces faced each other in a line of trenches that stretched across Belgium and northern France to neutral Switzerland. For three years, the lines scarcely moved, though millions died in the attempts to push the other side back.

The advantage lay with the defense. Men clambering out of the trenches were hit with machine-gun fire from the other trenches and artillery shells falling from above. Across their path lay coils of barbed wire. These were suicidal missions. Only in the last year of the war did the tank—a British invention—give attackers some protection.

The war would be won by the side that could last longest in supplying men

Total war: women munitions workers in Britain in World War I.

and metal to this killing machine. Whole economies had to be organized to supply the war; whole peoples had to be marshaled to fight, work, and believe in the cause. This was total war.

The British navy blockaded Germany to deny it goods from overseas. The German navy sent its submarines—U-boats—to sink ships supplying Britain with goods and, most important, with food. It had to exercise some care. The United States remained neutral; if Germany sank its ships, that would risk bringing it into the war. In February 1917, Germany, desperate to break the deadlock in the fighting, ordered unrestricted submarine warfare. It knew this would bring the United States into the war—it did in April 1917—but before American troops reached Europe, the plan was that Britain would be starving and the war won. The emperor and his chancellor were doubtful about this decision but the military was now in control. Generals Hindenburg and Ludendorff were in effect the government of Germany. Later, they had close dealings with Hitler. Ludendorff supported him in a failed coup in 1923. Hindenburg appointed him chancellor in 1933.

Germany enrages the United States: the sinking of the *Lusitania*, which was carrying American citizens and munitions from New York to Liverpool.

Then the Germans had a stroke of good fortune. Revolution broke out in Russia. Tsar Nicholas II abdicated. The new government planned to fight on in the war, but the Germans knew that Lenin, the Russian communist leader, was opposed to the war. He was living in exile in Switzerland. The German government organized to transport him across Germany in a sealed train so that he could return to Russia. There, he did what they had hoped—took Russia out of the war. Such are the desperate measures that war impels. The government of German generals was responsible for communism's first success, if we assume, what is quite reasonable, that without Lenin the Bolsheviks would not have won power.

To get Russia out of the war, Lenin had to agree to very harsh terms from Germany, which claimed huge swaths of western Russia. Now Germany was free to concentrate all its force on the western front. Early in 1918, it made one last assault, which pushed the French and British back but did not break them. They then counterattacked with the help of American soldiers, who arrived in greater numbers sooner than the Germans had expected. The Germans were now in full-scale retreat. In August, the generals knew that the war was lost.

President Woodrow Wilson had a hard task taking his country to war. There was a strong tradition of the United States' keeping clear of the entanglements and wars of Europe. The president turned the war into one that Americans could more readily support by declaring that it was not to be a war of conquest and vengeance; it was a war to make the world "safe for democracy." Future peace would be assured by subjected ethnic groups becoming separate nations; secret treaties between nations would end; and there would be a new world body to settle disputes. Wilson's principles for the peace were listed in Fourteen Points.

Facing defeat, the German generals thought it would be better to appeal to Wilson for peace rather than Britain and France, which were bent on vengeance. Realizing correctly that Wilson would not want to deal with a Germany run by generals, they told William II that he should now introduce proper parliamentary government, with a chancellor and ministers responsible to the Reichstag. So what the liberals had failed to achieve since 1848 was delivered by the military high command. Wilson was not altogether persuaded by the sudden change; he thought the "military masters and monarchical autocrats" were still in charge. Wilson wanted the emperor to go; for the moment, he refused.

After the revolution from above came a revolutionary threat from below. Now that it was clear that the war was lost, German sailors and soldiers mutinied and workers went on strike. They formed councils with a mixture of demands, but they all wanted the war to stop and the emperor to go. The inspiration of the councils was the Russian soviets, and Russia was the model for socialists who wanted to use the councils for a workers' revolution. Bolshevism terrified everyone else. The savagery of communist rule in Russia was well known. It had attacked not only property-holders but other reforming and socialist parties—such as the German Social Democratic Party. Stopping the spread of Russian communism was to be one of Hitler's great drawing cards. Yet it was from Bolshevik rule in Russia that he learned what revolutionary movements could achieve when they threw off all restraints on the exercise of power.

William II's last chancellor was convinced that two things were necessary to prevent revolution: The emperor must abdicate and the Social Democrats must be put in power. So the emperor went into exile and Friedrich Ebert, the leader of the Social Democrats, became chancellor. Ebert was still committed to socialism but he wanted it to be achieved through regular parliamentary means, not by revolution that could end in terror and civil war, to which he and his colleagues would likely fall victim. The revolutionary socialists put to him that a new democratic Germany would amount to little if the great industrial combines, the army, the civil service, and the judges remained as they were before. But Ebert was never going to use force against them.

For a time, Ebert had to humor the workers' councils and rule with them, but when revolutionary socialists proclaimed socialist republics, which happened in several places in the chaos of the years after the war, Ebert moved firmly to suppress them. The army offered him full cooperation and killed many workers. When the soldiers were unwilling to fire on workers, the army and the Social Democratic defense minister organized informal forces called Free Corps, made up of officers and ex-soldiers who were eager to put down revolution. They did the job with a vengeance.

The revolutionary socialists and their followers never forgave Ebert and the Social Democrats for this betrayal of the socialist cause. They formed themselves into a Communist Party, the largest party outside Russia, and like other communist parties around the globe,

Free Corps troops about to execute a revolutionary socialist.

took direction from Moscow. The Communists won substantial representation in the Reichstag, achieving nothing except making the threat of Russian communism real and close at hand.

Meanwhile, the victorious powers were meeting in Paris to agree on a peace treaty. As best they could, they drew the boundaries for new nations in Eastern Europe, but this was not going to ensure peace because ethnicities were mixed and making countries viable was at odds with making their people of one sort. A League of Nations was established, which was handicapped from the start because the US Senate refused to allow the United States to join it. On Germany, President Wilson had to compromise: It was to be a very harsh peace. Germany lost territory in the east to create Poland; in the west, it lost Alsace and Lorraine. It was to have no military forces or equipment in a thirty-mile strip on its side of the Rhine. Its defense forces were to be severely limited in men and equipment. There was to be no air force. Large payments were to be made in reparation for the damage the war had caused. The peace treaty explicitly declared Germany guilty of starting the war.

Germany was not at the peace conference; these terms were presented to its government, which was told that it had to sign. The terms caused national outrage. To the dismay, disorientation and anger of defeat, there was now added a perpetual branding of guilt. It is true that Germany would have been as harsh, or more so, if it had won and that it was largely responsible for the outbreak of the war, but in treating Germany like this, the peace conference planted the seeds for the next war. Germany could not live with these restrictions and humiliations; one way or another it would have them rectified.

Before the war, the German working-class movement was large in numbers but weak in influence. How it was to be accommodated within the state was not yet clear. The twelve months after defeat in the war gave the answer. Social Democrats were thrust into power to kill the socialists who had opted for revolution and to assume responsibility for the national humiliation. They got no thanks for doing this dirty work from the middle and upper classes or from the army. Social Democrats actually came to be blamed for Germany's defeat. Hindenburg began the story that the politicians had stabbed the army in the back. This had some plausibility because when the fighting stopped, the army was in good order on French and Belgian soil. Hindenburg and Ludendorff were sure it was beaten; it was they who wanted the war stopped at that point for they feared if the French and British pushed on into Germany there would be revolution. But the "stab in the back" stuck; it was one of Hitler's great weapons. He called the Social Democrats the "November criminals."

THE GERMAN CONSTITUTION had been altered in a rush in October 1918 to please President Wilson. In January 1919, a constituent assembly was elected by the people to draw up a full constitution for the new republic. The assembly could not meet in Berlin because it was likely to be beset by strikes and attempts at socialist revolution; it met instead in the small city of Weimar, which gave its name to the new constitution and the republic it established. Threatened by revolution even before it began, this new democratic republic had an unusual feature: The president, to be elected by the citizens (men and women) every seven years, could in the event of disorder suspend basic human rights and use force to preserve the republic. The constituent assembly installed Ebert, the Social Democratic leader, as its first president. On several occasions he used this emergency power. Normally, government was in the hands of the chancellor, chosen by the president, who was required to have the support of a majority in the Reichstag.

Any new regime will struggle to gain legitimacy. The Weimar Republic had the great handicap of being associated with national defeat and humiliation. Furthermore, the enemies of the republic were, from the first, well established in the Reichstag itself. There was no consensus across the parties that this was the constitution that had to be made to work and that bound them all. On the left was the Communist Party openly advocating revolution to establish a Soviet Germany and taking its orders from the Soviet Union, as Russia was now called. On the right were conservative and nationalist parties that wanted to bring back the emperor, curb democracy, and overthrow the restrictions that the Versailles Treaty had imposed. In the middle ground were the Social Democrats, the Center Party (supported by Catholics), and the Democrats, a liberal middle-class party.

Two years after the Weimar Republic began, German society was thrown into chaos by hyperinflation, a rapid rise in prices that made money close to worthless. If you owed money, you could readily pay off your debts. If you held savings, as middle-class people did, they were destroyed. The government had to print more and more money and you needed a suitcase or a wheelbarrow to carry your money to the shops. After twelve months, the government stabilized the situation by starting a new currency, but the memory of a world out of control, of respectable people being ruined, lived on. At the next crisis, middle-class people were more ready to support desperate measures.

No party ever gained a majority of seats in the Reichstag. All governments had to be coalitions; chancellors had to find a majority somehow and regularly failed to do so as fragile coalitions broke apart. Party rivalry is never pretty, but strong government by a party with a majority has its attractions. Germans under Weimar never experienced that. It was easy for Hitler to denounce the republic for its permanent divisions and squabbles.

Burning money for warmth.

The Social Democrats, the largest party before the war, were seen as most likely to gain a majority, but they were impeded by the renewed fears of socialism stoked by communist rule in Russia and communist threats in Germany. For all their commitment to the republic, they had not renounced Marx, which meant they were not going to make gains outside the working class. A large slice of their working-class support now went to the Communist Party, which denounced Social Democrats as capitalist lackeys and refused to cooperate with them. Social Democrats and Communists were both opposed to Nazism but, divided as they were, they had less chance of stopping Hitler.

The Communists were so narrow-minded that, in the election for president after Ebert's death in 1925, they ran their own candidate, who of course had no chance of winning, rather than vote for the candidate agreed on by the Center Party and the Social Democrats. This gave the election to the candidate from the right: Hindenburg, the authoritarian conservative general who blamed politicians for Germany's defeat in the war and who, in 1933, would make Hitler chancellor.

FOR MOST OF THE 1920S, Hitler's party was on the margins. It was called the National Socialist Party, Socialist because he wanted to appeal to workers but National to mark it off from the internationalism of Marxian socialism. Hitler was enraged by Marx's claims that workers had no country, that their first loyalty should be to their class, and that they should divide their country by means of class warfare. The socialist content of the party's program was steadily watered down, and those who wanted to take it seriously were thrown out or, after Hitler was chancellor, killed. Hitler did not want to attack big business, which was to do the work of rearming Germany. But he wanted workers to have a job and live comfortably in better housing and with more vacations, though they were forbidden to have unions. He planned the production of the Volkswagen, the people's car, which in Hitler's time never reached the people; those that were made went into the army.

The program was much more National than Socialist. Hitler wanted an end to party division, to create a united Germany under his leadership, strong enough to overturn the restrictions of Versailles, to which the cowardly politicians had agreed, and to claim "living space" for the German nation to the east, occupied for the moment by the "inferior" Slavs: the Poles, Ukrainians, and Russians. The internal enemies of the Reich should be eliminated: These were Marxists, both socialists and communists, and, most importantly, the Jews. Hitler believed there was a worldwide Jewish conspiracy to debase the "higher" races that were the carriers of civilization. Marx was a Jew and some leading Bolsheviks in Russia were Jews, so Bolshevism became "Jewish Bolshevism." Hitler held the Jews responsible for World War I and mused how so much suffering could have been avoided if they had all been gassed.

There was an age-old prejudice against Jews in Europe as the killers of Christ. But as race-thinking became stronger in the nineteenth century, anti-Semites began to see Jews as an immediate and insidious threat to racial health. Jews interbreeding with the higher races would damage their prospects in the struggle of existence. These ideas were widely shared and not just in Germany; they were defended as "scientific"; Hitler was unusual in being so paranoid about the alleged danger and so absolutely inhuman in seeking a solution for it.

Hitler was not the founder of the Nazi Party. Under the name German Workers' Party, it began in Munich in southern Germany in January 1919. Hitler attended his first meeting a few months later and was surprised to find that though the party was against parliamentary democracy, it made decisions by voting. He soon showed them different. He became the unquestioned leader, banned committees, and ruled that the party platform was never to be debated again. This power fell to him because of his extraordinary ability as a speaker; he could entrance, persuade, excite,

and energize his audiences.
This demobilized soldier,
who had been a dropout and
drifter before the war, had
found his metier. His abilities
made this minuscule party
into a significant player in
Munich's political life and
won Hitler the support of
some influential people.

Adolf Hitler: master of oratory.

In 1923, Hitler planned with some support from local army
units and the backing of General Ludendorff to march on Berlin
with his followers and unseat the government. This was in imitation of Mussolini's March on Rome, which led to his becoming dictator of Italy in 1922. Mussolini's movement called itself
fascist after the bundle of sticks (*fasces*), which were the symbol of
authority in ancient Rome. The fascists aimed to put down division, especially class division fostered by the workers, and build
national strength under the control of a strongman or dictator.

Hitler admired Mussolini's fascism but his attempt to imitate
Mussolini's seizure of power was a dreadful failure; the police
were enough to stop it. There was a brief exchange of gunshots;
four police and fourteen of Hitler's men were killed. Hitler was
put on trial for treason and, like other right-wing nationalist
rebels in Weimar's disturbances, got a light sentence—five years'
imprisonment—because he was seen as acting for patriotic reasons.
The socialist and communist rebels usually did not get trials; they
were shot. Ludendorff, to his own disgust, was declared innocent.

Hitler was confined not in a jail but comfortably in an old
castle used for political prisoners. He had the leisure to read, think,
and write. He produced a long rambling book called *Mein Kampf*
(*My Struggle*), which became the Bible of his movement. It was a
hodgepodge of his life story, his political views, and the history
and future of racial struggles. None of the ideas were original; the

original passages recorded his discoveries on how to get a crowd to change its mind, what he called "mass suggestion" and "mass effect." Speaking was crucial; print was too cool a medium. Reasoning would not work; you meet set views and habit and you have to overwhelm them; your will must prevail over the multitude of individual wills. The time and setting for meetings were important: night rather than day; some halls would work and some would not. Later, Hitler graduated from Munich beer halls to presiding over huge outdoor rallies, very carefully staged and choreographed. He knew why they worked: The lone, uncertain individual becomes part of a larger community and the morale of the community soars.

Hitler boasted in his book of his success in beating the communists who came to break up his meetings. Getting police protection was a mistake. It was important to show that the movement could look after itself. This was the origin of Hitler's storm troopers, dressed in brown shirts, his muscle at meetings and on the streets, which grew into a huge private army. He was contemptuous of the middle class, who hated communists but did not know how to deal with them: "terror can only be broken by terror."

Hitler was freed in less than a year. He announced that he was putting illegal methods behind him; his movement would come to power in a constitutional way, but he made no secret that once he was in power the constitution would be very different, not parties contesting for power, but one party, with himself, the Führer, in charge. And on his way to power, he wielded the threat of force: his storm troopers, always keen for action. As a sign that force was his mode, Hitler always carried a dog whip.

The Nazi Party attracted people from all classes: workers, clerks, shopkeepers, students, farmers, and middle-class and upper-class people. The other parties represented a class or a faith or a region; the Nazi Party alone was truly national and gained in strength because none of the others ever could be that. Hitler did not run it as a political party; it was a dynamic national movement staking its claim to take charge of the nation. Within the party, its highly diverse members were of equal standing, which was a novel practice in a society still very status-conscious. Members were equal in their love of country, their membership of the superior Aryan race, and their obedience to the Führer, who was, as the party propaganda trumpeted, an ordinary man.

HAD THE GREAT DEPRESSION not occurred and not affected Germany so badly, the Nazis would almost certainly have remained a group of no great consequence. In 1930, the second year of the Depression, the government (as always, a coalition) broke up. Its Social Democratic members refused to agree to a lowering of unemployment benefits, on which millions now relied. It was a disastrous stand on principle. An election followed in which the Nazis made spectacular gains, from 2.6 percent of the vote at the previous election to 18.3 percent. At the next election, in 1932, in the depth of the Depression, they gained 37.3 percent of the vote and became the largest party in the Reichstag. The Nazi vote grew first at the expense of the nationalists on the right, then from the middle-class parties in the center. The combined vote of the working-class parties, the Social Democrats, and the Communists, held up well; their followers were not lured to Hitler. But about one in four workers did vote for him in 1932; these came mostly from smaller towns and the country. Hitler had cross-class support.

From 1930, President Hindenburg used his emergency powers to support governments because no government could get a majority in the Reichstag. The Social Democrats would not support cuts to social security; the Communists and Nazis would support only themselves. The president and those around him began to think of ways to establish authoritarian government that would not depend on the Reichstag and that would take the necessary harsh measures to deal with the economic crisis and prevent a revolt of the unemployed, whom the Communists were busy recruiting. Large landholders, the army, and parts of big business were urging the president to limit or shut down democracy.

A majority could be found in the Reichstag if the Nazis ruled in coalition with other nationalist parties on the right, but Hitler insisted that he would join no government unless he were chancellor. He had promoted himself as the nation's leader; he was not going to be, he could not be, a mere minister or deputy. Hindenburg swore he would never make such an intolerant man chancellor. But finally, the popular support that Hitler could bring to an authoritarian government could not be ignored. The danger of Hitler as chancellor was to be met by allowing only three Nazis to be ministers; the rest came from other nationalist parties who would keep Hitler in check. What a miscalculation! The Nazis were so ruthless in using the power they acquired, and Hitler was soon so popular, that the old politicians were marginalized. President Hindenburg was a restraining force. When he died in 1934, Hitler made himself president as well as chancellor.

The Nazi dictatorship was established with the appearance of legality. The plan was to get the Reichstag to pass a law allowing the government itself to make laws—and so making the Reichstag irrelevant. A two-thirds vote was needed for such a constitutional change. Upon taking office, Hitler demanded and got from the president an early election so that the Nazis could boost their Reichstag numbers. Just before polling day, a Dutch communist set fire to the Reichstag building. Hitler declared that this was the beginning of a communist attempt to seize power and persuaded the president to use his emergency powers to suspend civil and political liberties. The Communist Party was banned and communists were taken away to concentration camps. Even so, the Nazis did not gain a majority—they got 43.9 percent of the vote. They needed the support of the nationalist parties and the Catholic Center Party to carry their Enabling Bill. The Center Party, whose electoral support had held up against the Nazi advance, reluctantly agreed after receiving verbal assurances, which were broken, about the independence of the churches. Only the Social Democrats courageously voted against. The Communist deputies were already locked away or had fled. Storm troopers stood around the hall to intimidate the members as the votes were taken. The government used its new powers to ban first the Social Democratic Party and then all others. Only the Nazi Party was legal.

The elimination of the Marxist parties had been done promptly. This, above all, was what those who had engineered an authoritarian government had wanted.

On the Jews, which was Hitler's fixation, the Nazi government moved more cautiously. The storm troopers took their own direct action and had to be restrained. Boycotts of Jewish businesses appalled many people and caused economic disruption and were called off. Then, by law in 1935, Jews were deprived of citizenship and forbidden to marry or have sexual relations with Germans. In 1938, the Nazis gave the signal to their followers for an attack on Jewish shops, businesses, and synagogues. This was Kristallnacht, the Night of Broken Glass. For the first time, Jews were sent to concentration camps because they were Jews rather than members of political organizations. Then a return to "legality": Laws were issued that took property from Jews, kept them out of public places, and expelled their children from school. Emigration of Jews was encouraged. What form their complete elimination would take had not yet been decided.

Within a few years of taking office, Hitler had fulfilled his promise to overturn the restrictions of the Versailles Treaty. He reintroduced conscription for the armed services and planned an army five times larger than Versailles had stipulated. He started an airforce. He marched German troops into the demilitarized Rhineland. Britain and France were not willing to risk war to stop him. They did not want to revisit the horrors of World War I, and, especially in Britain, there was a feeling that the peace treaty had been too harsh and Germany should be allowed to make up ground. This was the policy of appeasement: Allow Germany what was reasonable and Hitler's aggression would cease. Or as Winston Churchill, the most ferocious British opponent of appeasement, said: "An appeaser is one who feeds a crocodile—hoping it will eat him last."

In German-speaking Austria, there was strong support for a Nazi party that wanted Austria to amalgamate with Germany. The Versailles Treaty had carved new nations out of the old Austro-Hungarian Empire and left a much-reduced Austria for the German speakers. But they were forbidden by the treaty to join Germany. Hitler was determined to include them. The Austrian chancellor, under pressure from the local Nazis, decided to hold a referendum on the question. Before it was held, Hitler marched his soldiers in and was received with rapture in Vienna—and in Germany, when he returned.

The popularity that came to Hitler on overturning the restrictions of Versailles showed how deep was the humiliation they had caused. Some people had been prepared to bear them until better times; others had wanted to challenge them immediately; and now suddenly, they were lifted and Germans of all sorts, those who voted for Hitler and those against, were united in pride at the revival of the nation into a great power. Later, when Hitler was scoring defeats rather than triumphs, he was not so popular, but he already had the apparatus to deal with any resisters: They were eliminated by the secret police, the Gestapo, or disappeared into the concentration camps.

In the new states of Czechoslovakia and Poland, created by the Versailles Treaty, there were communities of Germans whom Hitler claimed for Germany. France and Britain were pledged to protect Czechoslovakia, but when Hitler threatened war to incorporate the German Czechs into the Reich, France and Britain crumpled and told Czechoslovakia to give way. Because he had kept the peace, the British prime minister, Neville Chamberlain, went home from Germany to a hero's welcome. Hitler declared that he had no more territorial claims in Europe, but Chamberlain speeded up Britain's defense preparations.

When Hitler invaded Poland in September 1939, Britain and France at last declared war on Germany. To ensure that he did not have a war on two fronts, Hitler concluded a nonaggression pact with the communist Soviet Union, the country he loathed as the home of the Jewish Bolshevik poison. This time, the German plans to conquer France worked; it was defeated in five weeks by a blitzkrieg, "lightning war," where troops protected by tanks on the ground and planes above rolled rapidly over the enemy.

Britain stood alone against Hitler. Plans for invasion were drawn up, but first, Germany had to gain control of the skies. This was the Battle of Britain, which was narrowly won by the British pilots. Churchill, now British prime minister, said of them: "Never in the field of human conflict was so much owed by so many to so few." Hitler was puzzled that Britain would not accept the deal he offered: Britain could keep control of its worldwide empire if it left Germany free to control Europe. He put it down to the influence of "Jewish plutocracy." With Britain undefeated, Hitler turned east to attack the Soviet Union, which meant he would eventually have a war on two fronts. A mistake, by narrow military calculation, but Hitler was not going to leave "Jewish Bolshevism" to thrive and on land that was needed to give Germany "living space." That Hitler would destroy Russian communism did make him attractive to some people in ruling circles in Britain who were tempted by the deal Hitler offered. But not, of course, Churchill.

Hitler did not think there would be a war on two fronts because he was confident he would defeat Russia in five months. That was his big miscalculation. Blitzkrieg did not work so well in the vast Russian distances and against an enemy that had huge reserves of manpower. Stalin, the Russian dictator, had by relentless control and terror industrialized the backward country that the communists had seized, which meant his forces could be supplied with tanks, planes, and artillery to match the Germans'. The

Germans made huge inroads into Russia, but the Russian armies fell back, and at Stalingrad, in February 1943, surrounded and took into captivity a whole German army. Hitler had not allowed the Germans to retreat or surrender when the battle was clearly lost. From then on, the Russians were on the offensive. It took them over two years to reach Berlin.

For Hitler, the conflict in the east was much more than war; he made it into a crusade of mass murder and enslavement so that the lands of Slavs and Jews would be open to settlement by the master race. The Jews were at first rounded up and shot but, as this was slow and distasteful work, the Nazis constructed a factory-like killing machine in which Jews were gassed and their bodies burned in ovens. Once this system was operating, Jews were brought from all the lands the Nazis had occupied to be destroyed. The collection and transport of Jews went on even as the fighting was going against Hitler and his resources were seriously stretched. For Hitler, the elimination of Jews had become top priority, necessary to secure Germany's future and a fit punishment for the race that, in his eyes, had caused this war as they had done the last. Overall, about six million Jews died in what has been named the Holocaust. Though the Nazis thought this destruction was for the best, they did not advertise what they were doing. But many thousands of Germans inside and outside the Nazi Party did know of it because they were directly involved.

The ovens at Dachau concentration camp.

Hitler's belief in a worldwide Jewish conspiracy helps to explain another of his military "mistakes." The United States did not enter the war until Japan, an ally of Germany, launched an attack on the US Navy at Pearl Harbor in Hawaii in December 1941. President Roosevelt, naturally, declared war on Japan, but aware of the still strong feeling in America against being involved in European conflict, he did not declare war on Germany. But Hitler immediately declared war on the United States, and so made an enemy of the world's greatest power. In doing so, he denounced President Roosevelt as being backed by the "entire satanic insidiousness" of Jews. To defeat the Jews, Hitler had to fight the United States.

President Roosevelt had long seen Hitler's Germany as a threat to the United States, though the majority of his countrymen could not. Now that the United States was in the war, Roosevelt and Churchill agreed that they would defeat Hitler first and run a holding war against the Japanese. So the majority of the forces that landed in German-occupied France in 1944 belonged to the United States, and an American (General Dwight Eisenhower) was in command.

Hitler now had a war on two fronts. Though the war was clearly lost, his troops fought resolutely to the end. American troops coming from the west and Russian troops from the east met in Germany in April 1945. It was the Russians who fought their way into the center of Berlin, where Hitler and his circle were sheltering in a bunker. Hitler was unmoved by the devastation that his war had brought to Germany. The fault lay with the German people, who had failed him and were unworthy to survive. He committed suicide rather than be captured.

Germany's Nazis fit a European pattern—and they were also unique. Democracy failed in almost all the countries of Europe between the wars and was replaced by fascist and authoritarian regimes. Representative government, let alone democracy, had shallow roots; and democracy had to make its way in some nations that were absolutely new—creations of the Versailles Treaty. But the Nazis were a more explosive and destructive force because they controlled the greatest European power, which had reason to be vengeful, and because they were under the control of Hitler, an evil genius without parallel. That such a man could come to power is understandable; that he could carry through his determination to eliminate the Jews seems almost beyond understanding, so that the Holocaust continues to challenge and horrify us.

HITLER NOT ONLY failed to destroy Russian communism; he had brought the Red Army into Central Europe. The Russians installed communist governments in the lands they had liberated from the Nazis: Poland, Czechoslovakia, Hungary, and the Balkan states, except Greece. Germany was divided between a communist east and a democratic capitalist west. In 1946, Churchill spoke of an "iron curtain" that now divided Europe.

In 1951, another barrier began to come down. Germany and France, the old enemies, agreed to pool their resources of coal and iron and avoid being competitors in the making of steel. From this beginning came the European Common Market (1958), which was a grouping of six European countries with France and Germany at its core. These economic arrangements were the way Germany was accepted back into the community of nations and tied into peaceful relations with them. Economic cooperation grew into the European Union (1993), a political organization that was a European federation in the making.

In the later 1980s, when the Soviet Union began to reform itself and would no longer support the communist regimes of Eastern Europe, those regimes quickly collapsed. The ex-communist countries applied to join the European Union and were accepted. The collapse of communist regimes freed millions of people from tyranny and freed Europe finally from the poisonous doctrine that its civilization was simply a system of oppression and that a ruthless dictatorship would create a workers' state of perfect equality.

How much authority will be given to the European Union is still a matter of contention. The union in itself is a way of controlling the nationalism that fostered war, but can a state operate if there is no common feeling to sustain it? Can a European spirit develop to sustain a full European federation?

In 2004, the member states drew up a formal constitution, a single document to replace the treaties under which the union had operated, and which was to make it more cohesive. All members had to accept it before it came into operation. The process fell apart when the French and Dutch people rejected the constitution in referendums. Another treaty had to be created to do some of what the constitution had intended. The union may have also overreached by creating a common currency—the euro—without there being a central government to take responsibility for it.

The constitution of the European Union, so far not adopted, in the usual way carries a preamble. In a civilization of mixed origins there was naturally argument over what it should contain. The pope wanted Christianity acknowledged; the Germans would have accepted this but France, the home and nurturer of Enlightenment, was fiercely opposed. So it is not Christianity that is acknowledged, but more vaguely, Europe's religious inheritance, which is joined to the humanism from the Renaissance and to its culture generally. Enlightenment is the dominant influence, for a Europe committed to "the universal values of the inviolable and inalienable rights of the human person" is to follow the path of "progress and prosperity." And nationalism will be transcended, for "while remaining proud of their own national identities and history, the peoples of Europe are determined to transcend their former divisions and, united ever more closely, to forge a common destiny."

Afterword

by Filip Slaveski, PhD

John Hirst ended his *Shortest History of Europe* on an optimistic note. In 2004, the European Union (EU) had just expanded to include a number of Eastern European countries, formerly behind the Iron Curtain, marking a "victory" of European unity after a terrible twentieth century of division. This new unified Europe was committed to the "universal values of the inviolable and inalienable rights of the human person," the EU said, and while remaining "proud of their own national identities," Europeans would transcend nationalism and grow into an ever-closer Union toward "progress and prosperity." Hirst reminded us, however, that the EU's platitudes about "unity" emerged as a result of the impasse among member states over acknowledging Christianity as a core European value in the preamble to the (unadopted) 2004 EU constitution. The impasse over this specific question stumbled over deeper divisions in European history concerning identity and national sovereignty that would shape the EU's, indeed, the entire continent's existential crises over the next two decades, especially between its "eastern" and "western" parts. In fact, identity and national sovereignty have shaped the eurozone crisis from 2009 to the mid-2010s, the following refugee crisis in 2015, Brexit in 2016, and the EU's response to Russia's war on Ukraine since 2014. In this way, Hirst's Shortest History is relevant and insightful in also understanding the key story of European history after its publication.

Hirst was also correct to be wary about the EU's adoption of a common currency, the euro, without a central government to take responsibility for it, leaving it to the European Central Bank (ECB). The eurozone crisis threatened EU economies and exacerbated tensions among EU member states and especially with the ECB and Brussels, the seat of major EU institutions. The massive austerity measures inflicted by Brussels on the national economies of EU member states to deal with the crisis squeezed the slim pockets of many ordinary citizens and brought into sharp relief the power of largely unaccountable "far away technocrats" to make (often pernicious) decisions about their daily lives. The EU's handling of the refugee crisis from 2015, allowing millions of refugees to enter EU countries, exacerbated this sense of powerlessness for many. Already grim social welfare structures strained further under growing population pressures, and the composition of societies changed more rapidly.

Unsurprisingly, popular responses to these crises of decreasing living standards and massive demographic and social change have threated EU unity. The United Kingdom removed itself from the EU by plebiscite in 2016, the first time a member state has left the Union. While the reasons for the majority of Britons supporting Brexit remain contested, poverty, migration, and sovereignty were undoubtedly major factors. The second major source of disunity has come from within the EU itself, from the so-called "new Europe" in the "East," incorporated in 2004. Right-wing populist rebellions in Poland and Hungary have gained enormous momentum in recent years, fueled by grievances among Hungarians and Poles against the EU.

The danger posed to EU unity by these rebellions is arguably much deeper than Brexit. In the eyes of many in Brussels, at least, the rebellions threaten the core shared values of European society: liberalism, democracy, individual rights, and political pluralism.

Both Law and Justice and Fidesz, the ruling parties in Poland and Hungary respectively, are democratically elected governments that have been widely seen as dismantling liberal democracy in their countries, especially by diminishing the independence of the judiciary in Poland and attacking political opponents in Hungary. Fidesz's leader, Prime Minister Viktor Orbán, has specifically stated he is committed to creating a "Christian illiberal democracy." As with Law and Justice's vision of a traditional Polish Catholic society, it is clearer what this program excludes than what it includes. Neither regime wants the mass migration of non-Christians, especially Muslims, to their country, and neither supports minority sexual rights—both major EU initiatives. Poland and Hungary are wresting power back from Brussels (using billions of euros of EU funding), to support national and religious programs inimical to the EU's supranational and secular order. The 2004 impasse about recognizing Christianity as a root of European civilization in the Constitution's preamble reflects these deeper problems. They will likely endure.

Hirst had little room in his Shortest History for Poland, Hungary, and Eastern Europe because, he jibed, he was writing the *Shortest History of Europe* and the partition of Poland was not as important as the Renaissance. It was not, but to return the jibe, the Polish/Hungarian challenge to the EU has been central in shaping more recent European history. Russia's partition of Ukraine by annexing Crimea in 2014, together with the potential for further partition as a consequence of the current war, may be the most pressing problem confronting Europe's immediate future. To further advance Hirst's Shortest History to today, we need to more seriously take the "East" into account. Indeed, we should consider what these categories of "Eastern" and "Western" Europe mean today.

Hirst's "Western Europe" *was* Europe. He argued it came about over centuries of conflict among small powers who traced their origins to the melding of the Greek, Roman, and Germanic worlds. Kings ruled but were never absolute. They relied on nobles to prop them up by collecting their taxes and providing troops to defend their kingdoms against other kings, to whom the nobles could swap allegiance. The incessant conflict among kings and their relationship with nobles formed the competitive and cooperative wellspring of political structures aided by the Reformation and Enlightenment that would form—and eventually come to characterize—much of what many people understand of "modern" Europe. This Europe was composed of nation-states run by representative democracies and framed by the rule of law and legally protected individual rights.

Hirst's "Eastern Europe" was more similar to Asia than Western Europe. Consisting implicitly of the Byzantine, Russian, and Ottoman Empires, it had been run largely by absolutist monarchs who, in the absence of internecine warfare and with less reliance on their nobility, had less incentive to modernize their kingdoms and share power within them. The "East" formed from a different wellspring, which produced the society of Eastern Europe. It benefited less from the great intellectual movements of the West and the "modern" social, economic, and political development they spawned, earning its "backward" reputation.

We should not dismiss this perceived dichotomy between the "modern" West and "backward" East simply because it is historically questionable. "Backward" (i.e., rural) Eastern Europe housed some of the greatest industrial regions of the nineteenth century.[1] Many scholars now understand this dichotomy not as an organic historical development, but as a creation by Enlightenment thinkers who imagined their Western Europe as "modern" by imagining its antithesis in "backward" Eastern Europe.[2] This dichotomy remains important despite its inaccuracies because it continues to permeate European thinking about what Europe is and especially where it ends. EU officials in Brussels who speak endlessly of "more Europe," that is, a bigger EU with more members in a more united supranational body, are often at odds with politicians in national capitals of Western Europe who see things differently. Alongside all the formal discussions and bureaucratic processes associated with integrating Eastern European countries like Ukraine or those in the Western Balkans to the EU, they are seen as beyond Europe or, given their history, just not European "enough"—or not yet—for full EU membership.

The criteria Hirst listed as the staple characteristics of modern Western states—rule of law, individual rights—are not seen as organic to Eastern Europe. Yet, they are the goalposts by which Eastern countries are measured for their "Europeanness" and candidacy for membership. For EU optimists, the successful eastward expansion from 2004 onward demonstrates the potential for overcoming these East/West divisions.[3] For cynics, the Polish/Hungarian challenge to the EU, often rejecting these criteria, tempers this optimism. The experience of Ukraine between the first Russian invasion in 2014 and the next in 2022, when the EU's initial enthusiasm about Ukrainian membership stumbled quickly in the reality of accession politics, confirms for cynics that the goalposts shift forward every time these countries make advances. North Macedonia waited seventeen years, from 2005 to 2022, to proceed from candidate status to actual negotiations on EU accession. There are many reasons why it had to wait so long—its neighbors vetoing its accession, for one—reflecting deeper complexities in Balkan politics. But Macedonia still has little prospect of gaining full membership anytime soon—or perhaps ever. There is no decisive united push among EU heavyweight countries supporting its accession or for other "complex" cases, constraining the European future of Eastern Europe to Western perceptions of historical "backwardness."

Long the subject of endless debate by European scholars and EU commentators, these questions about where Europe starts and ends, how big the EU should be, and who is European or at least a "good" European have now developed deadly consequences with Russia's war on Ukraine, especially after Russia's all-out invasion of the country in February 2022. This invasion poses the greatest test for EU unity since its existential crises of the 2010s, forcing both a major rethink of these questions and the EU's axiom of having superseded nation-state conflict in Europe through its integration and cooperation polices, including toward Russia. The EU rethought this axiom quickly as approximately 150,000 Russian troops invaded Ukraine. Putin echoed Hitler's baseless justification for the invasion of Czechoslovakia to protect Sudeten Germans in 1938 when attributing the invasion to, among other things, stopping the "genocide" of Russian-speakers in the Donbas. As thousands of Ukrainian civilians perish under Russian guns, Ukraine has widely been seen as defending not only itself but democracy and European values against the barbarism of Vladimir Putin's Russia. This moment is very different from Russia's initial invasion of the Donbas in 2014 by "proxy forces," which enabled it to deny its war against Ukraine and provided a pretext for European leaders to avoid direct confrontation with Russia. In 2022, almost overnight, the EU started to speak of Ukraine not as the "East," but as the new European frontier against the new "East" of Putin's barbarism, now led under the staunchly pro-European popular elected government of President Volodymyr Zelenskyy. Czech Prime Minister Petr Fiala stressed, "Ukrainians were fighting for us too."[4] German Chancellor Olaf Sholz extrapolated "us" to mean the EU. He argued that the Ukrainian case reflected the core principle upon which the EU was founded, that a rules-based order should prevail over the "might makes right" principle responsible for the catastrophes of European history.

> The issue at the heart of this is whether power is allowed to prevail over the law. Whether we permit Putin to turn back the clock to the nineteenth century and the age of the great powers. Or whether we have it in us to keep warmongers like Putin in check.[5]

Germany acted to do exactly that when it reversed its decades-old restrictions on providing military aid to other countries, adding to the billions-worth of EU and American arms given to Ukraine to defend itself. In June 2022, all leaders of EU member states seemed to share this commitment to "law" and supported the EU Commission's recommendation to unanimously support Ukrainian candidacy to EU membership. It may be that now the EU has managed to decisively

> break through the old pattern [since 2014], in which they had done enough to strengthen the motivation of Ukrainians to fight for democracy and national independence, while denying them sufficient support to enable them to defy Russia.[6]

The unprecedented level of support for Ukraine, militarily, financially, and otherwise, may culminate in a much-discussed EU-US "Marshall Plan for Ukraine," that will rebuild the county in the same way that the original Marshall plan rebuilt Western Europe after WWII and helped it achieve its postwar prosperity. If this continued support for Ukraine breaks the old pattern from 2014, the EU and Ukraine might come through the war as stronger and more united entities, as the EU did, its optimists argue, from the crises of the 2010s.[7] Might Ukraine shift from the figurative to the actual new frontier against the "East" of Putin's Russia as a member of the EU, as the majority of Ukrainians and many Europeans now desire? In Ukraine itself, has Putin's war not pushed more Ukrainians toward Europe by his indiscriminate bombings, especially in eastern Ukraine, where the traditionally strong sympathies and cultural ties to Russia have diminished as a result?

All this may well happen, as most would hope, at the time of this writing, if any sort of justice were to prevail for Ukraine. Finishing this afterword on a similarly optimistic note, as Hirst did in his Shortest History, we should qualify it in the same way. It is becoming clear that the EU's support for Ukraine may threaten to break apart the very unity among member states that inspires its present solidarity. The EU's massive economic sanctions against Russia are damaging its economies as well. The EU's ban on the majority of Russian oil and gas imports, which fuels much of the

EU economy, was enacted before replacement sources could be found, leading to skyrocketing energy prices and exacerbating inflation. Hungary has already opted out of this blanket ban to continue its commitment to buying Russian fossil fuels. This is not to mention the billions of euros necessary to support over five million Ukrainian refugees still displaced in EU countries by the war. Support for Ukraine may falter then on the same fault lines of the eurozone and migrant crises of the 2010s. Faltering is likely as the conflict protracts and the war turns from an existential conflict for Ukraine to a war of attrition—not Ukraine defending itself from all-out invasion but launching counteroffensives to liberate eastern territories contested since Russia's first invasion in 2014. If there was little likelihood of the US and NATO providing troops to help defend Ukraine again Russia, it is less likely now. Is a new pattern emerging, then, in the EU's conduct toward Ukraine and Russia, where its support for Ukraine helps it to defy but not to defeat Russia? Might not the resultant continuation of the conflict further diminish Ukraine and the EU's capacity to support it?

These old and new patterns, in 2014 and in 2022, might end up being remarkably similar. As in 2022, there was much optimism at first about Ukraine's future in Europe in 2014, when Euro-maidan protests toppled its pro-Russian Yanukovych government. The revolution, though years in the making, was sparked by the government's decision to settle on a cooperation agreement with Russia instead of the EU. Russia responded to the revolution by attacking Ukraine by proxy forces in the Donbas and annexing Crimea. This inspired a wave of Ukrainian patriotism that bolstered optimism for breaking free of a Soviet/Russian shadow into the "light" of Europe. This optimism appeared to be reciprocated by many in Brussels, judging by their positive pronouncements about supporting Ukraine's membership to the EU. It was an uncanny moment, not because the drive for European integration was new in Ukraine nor because the EU had made no positive pronouncements about it before. Ukraine's Orange Revolution in

2005 was the watershed moment in this respect. It was uncanny because it occurred to me and many others on the streets of Kyiv that the cynicism that weighed so heavily on Ukrainian attitudes toward politics lifted in tandem with Brussels's cynicism toward the suitability of Ukraine as an EU member.[8] In the midst of the eurozone crisis, where EU unity was faltering, and support for leaving the EU grew among national populations, many in Brussels were inspired by Ukrainians flying EU flags, fighting, and, in some cases, dying on the streets of Kyiv under the Yanukovych government's fire to join Europe.

But the cynicism soon returned, and the optimism faltered in Ukraine and the EU as war strained Ukraine's economy and broader society and Europe lost interest in supporting Ukraine to liberate Crimea and its Donbas region after 2014. The EU eased its sanctions against Russia gradually afterward, returning very much to business as usual. German Chancellor Angela Merkel's conclusion of the Nord Stream II pipeline agreement with Putin vastly increased Germany's dependence on Russia for gas supplies. By rerouting Russian gas pipelines to Europe around Ukraine, it also removed Ukraine's strategic capacity to disrupt the flow of gas in response to Russian aggression as it continued to fight against Russia in the Donbas.[9] On the eve of all-out Russian invasion in February 2022, the EU's economic and strategic relationship with Russia had proved more important than its support for Ukraine. This appeasement likely emboldened President Putin to attack Ukraine and he very likely anticipate Europe will resume this policy.

The key challenge for Europe now is to distort Putin's calculation. It must somehow balance supporting Ukraine's fight against Russia and, at the same time, eventually broker a settlement between the sides as a way to begin restoring the cooperative and integrationist framework of maintaining peace it has practiced for decades. Europe must now fight for peace. This is an incredibly difficult challenge. Hirst's Shortest History gives every reason to believe Europe may resolve it, especially from his historical sense of the "European miracle"—how it came to dominate the world through, and sometimes as a result of, its catastrophes. EU optimists echo Hirst when they claim that the EU and Europe more broadly "fails forward."[10] The EU came through the existential crises in the 2010s to remain intact and emerge "even stronger." Like the dispute over the EU constitution in 2004, the deep problems of European history are unraveling before our eyes and tying Europe's future into new knots. Let us hope Europeans can untie them.

Filip Slaveski

Canberra, July 2022

FILIP SLAVESKI, PhD, is a professor of modern European history at Australian National University and the author of *Remaking Ukraine after WWII* and *The Soviet Occupation of Germany.*

1. Norman Davies, Europe: East and West (London: Jonathan Cape, 2006), 16.
2. Larry Wolff, "Voltaire's Public and the Idea of Eastern Europe: Toward a Literary Sociology of Continental Division," *Slavic Review* 54, no. 4, 1995.
3. Brigiid Laffan, "The next European century? Europe in global politics in the twenty-first century," *Journal of Contemporary European Research* 14, no. 4, 2018.
4. Stefan Auer, *European Disunion: Democracy, Sovereignty and the Politics of Emergency* (C. Hurst & Co. Publishers, 2022), 193.
5. Ibid., 189–90.
6. Ibid., 190.
7. E. Jones, R. D. Kelemen, and S. Meunier, "Failing Forward? Crises and Patterns of European Integration," *Journal of European Public Policy* 28, no. 10, 2021.
8. For a variety of Ukrainian and European reflections on the historical significance of Euromaidan on Ukraine's relationship to the EU and Europe more broadly, see Mykhailo Minakov, "The Significance of Euromaidan for Ukraine and Europe," *Focus Ukraine*, Kennan Institute, wilsoncenter.org/blog-post/the-significance-euromaidan-for-ukraine-and-europe.
9. The current German government has suspended the project as part of its sanctions package against Russian in response to Putin's invasion of Ukraine.
10. Jones, Kelemen, and Meunier, "Failing Forward?"

Image Credits

Index

About the Author

JOHN HIRST (1942–2016) was a celebrated historian and social commentator whose notable history books include *Australian History in Seven Questions* and *The Australians*. A history professor at La Trobe University for almost 40 years, he lived in Melbourne, Australia.

Also available in the Shortest History series

Trade Paperback Originals • $16.95 US | $21.95 CAN

978-1-61519-569-5

978-1-61519-820-7

978-1-61519-814-6

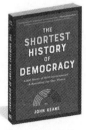

978-1-61519-896-2

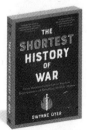

978-1-61519-930-3

978-1-61519-948-8

978-1-61519-950-1

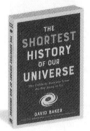

978-1-61519-973-0

978-1-61519-997-6